SIGNPOSTS

Direction For The Journey

Lois Williams

"Set up signposts, make landmarks,
set your heart toward the highway,
the way in which you went."
Jeremiah 31:21

May God bless your journey

Lois Williams

ISAIAH 30:21

Creative Force Press

Creative Force Press

SIGNPOSTS
By Lois Williams
www.LoveLettersFromLois.com

COPYRIGHT © 2018 by Lois Williams

This title is also available as an eBook. Visit
www.CreativeForcePress.com/titles for more information.

Published by Creative Force Press
4704 Pacific Ave, Suite C, Lacey, WA 98503
www.CreativeForcePress.com

Cover photo: Fredrick L. Williams, Copyright © 2018
Author Photo: Fredrick L. Williams. Copyright © 2018

ISBN: 978-1-939989-29-1

Printed in the United States

ENDORSEMENTS

In her warm, conversational style, Lois Williams provides welcoming signposts for the twists and turns of your life journey. Her heartfelt writings are filled with humor and honesty that will encourage you with their realness and point you to our God of hope. As she aptly writes, this book "marks the pause in the journey to remember and reflect on the ways God has touched my life and showed me Himself." As a reader, your life will be touched as well.

— Judy Gordon Morrow, author of *The Listening Heart: Hearing God in Prayer*

Gifted author and poet, Lois Williams, a courageous survivor of quadruple-bypass surgery, invites you into the personal pages of her journal and intimate relationship with God. As He healed her heart, both physically and spiritually, He gave her significant signposts — specific words from Scripture and life experience — to anchor her in hope, strength, and wisdom for life-changing recovery. Let God use this beautiful devotional to mark your own path, light your way, and direct you straight home to the heart of God.

— Lynn D. Morrissey, author of *Love Letters to God: Deeper Intimacy through Written Prayer* and Certified Journal Facilitator, CJF

An intimate journey into a Proverbs 31 woman's most defining moments. Told with unusual grace and poignancy, Signposts holds much wisdom and truth for those who also journey with the Lord through life's many hills and valleys. Be encouraged and blessed by the reading!

— Laura Frantz, Author

Another fantastic book by Lois Williams, *Signposts* is a great read for anyone who can relate to walking a tough road. Lois is consistently candid about the journey's ups and downs, and how God is always there to light the way.

—Krista Dunk, entrepreneur and author of *Step Out and Take Your Place* and *Kingdom Seeker's Devotional*

DEDICATION

To God, my Great Physician,
Who has healed
my body soul and spirit
with His Word
and to whom
belongs all the glory.

"Then they cried out to the LORD in their trouble, and
He saved them out of their distresses. He sent His word
and healed them." Psalm 107:19-20

FOREWORD

I hadn't been feeling very well for a month or so. Thinking it was the flu and a slow recovery, I was not prepared for what came next. A horrible headache and a spiraling blood pressure count headed me to the hospital. My heart was in crisis and I was in desperate need of bypass surgery! A quadruple bypass, it turned out to be, and I was in the hospital for 12 days.

I wondered what God was doing. Was He trying to get my attention? Drawing me to Himself? Yes. All of that. I feel Him asking me to share the story of my recovery and His work in my life. The result of that is *Signposts*. I hope that my story, to which many can relate, will be a help to you, precious reader, in whatever journey you are presently enduring.

This particular part of my life's journey began the day after Easter--surgery day, thus Easter will be a memorable day for our family for years to come. Through incredibly talented surgeons, sweet nurses, a group of prayer partners and an awesome loving God, our family has new life. In addition to celebrating a Risen Savior, we have experienced a beautiful reconciliation, giving us the blessing of a resurrected family.

And so, I open my heart to share my story with you.

INTRODUCTION

Loving to write and ponder my life, I spent a lot of time journaling my surgery recovery process, sharing it on a weekly basis with those who were faithfully reading my blog and praying with and for me. Unexpectedly, the next year involved more recovery from a total hip replacement (preceded by months of painful gout) and several other medical issues. All along I continued to write my thoughts.

There is a theme verse that initiated this book's title. Later I will explain how it came to me. It is Jeremiah 31:21, "Set up signposts, make landmarks; set your heart toward the highway, the way in which you went." Each week, as I pondered on paper, a word surfaced that touched my heart and seemed to identify the particular process of healing through which I was going. I would expand on the words as I wrote my blog posts.

Thus, *Signposts* is a compilation of those thoughts taken from my weekly blog over the period of April 2014 to April of 2016, written with my readers in mind. There were a few weeks, however, when I did not write or share. Sometimes I was either physically or emotionally unable to do so. It is a peek into those years of my life, very personal in nature. Though I have wondered if anyone would really be interested, I know that everyone is undertaking some sort of journey, and though mine is not any more fraught with pain and fear than anyone else's, my hope is that what God has made clear to me might be helpful to others.

It can be used as a devotional or read straight through as a story. I was writing from my actual experiences, so there are references to seasons, holidays, adventures, celebrations in my life. You will also find several of my poems included, most of which have been previously published in one of my devotional books: *Psalms From The Pathway, Heart Chords,* or *Pages.* Each segment represents one week of this journey, and though they are not always chronological, all were part of those years of recovery. Each segment is written around a one or two-word **SIGNPOST.**

Although I wrote these words for myself, directed to a specific group of readers, as time has passed it is my belief that God had you in mind as He poured the knowledge of His love through my pen. My hope is that within these pages you will find signposts for your own journey that will direct, strengthen and uphold you along the way.

LOVED

Hello Friends. A week has passed since returning home after surgery. Physically I am growing stronger and healing. Emotionally, well, that's another story. I am having a lot of trouble focusing and clarifying my thoughts. Journaling is difficult and I find I can't think of anything to say, for the most part. I am told this will get better; that it's all a process and I will once again be able to sort out my feelings. Apparently medication and anesthesia mess with my head! I do, though, try to spend some time writing as often as I can.

Earlier today I turned to Jeremiah 31:21 and found that it reached a place inside me. I feel that it is God's word to me this morning. It reads, "Set up signposts, make landmarks; set your heart toward the highway, the way in which you went." It seems to be a positive instruction, because I am truly at the start of a journey. What then will be the signposts, the landmarks? I pray that God will help me to perceive what their significance is to me in this odyssey to health--physical, emotional and spiritual.

I told the cardiac nurse when she asked me about my goal for rehab that I wanted to learn to care about myself. I had to admit that I never really have. I care desperately about being approved and acceptable, but taking care of myself was such a low priority it barely registered on the scale. It was arrogance in many ways, coupled with a weird low self-esteem, this feeling that no one would ever miss my presence on this earth. The outpouring of love and prayers I've received has stunned me.

Perhaps that should be the first signpost. **LOVED**. I am valuable, worthy of care. Valuable in the sight of my Heavenly Father who first breathed life into me. Valuable simply because of that. But also to my family and my friends.

What a shift in perspective! I can't really fathom it yet, nor absorb it. But I claim it today as the first milestone; the initial signpost. I am **LOVED**. Thank You, Heavenly Father.

"The LORD has appeared of old to me, saying: 'Yes, I have loved you with an everlasting love; therefore with lovingkindness I have drawn you.'" Jeremiah 31:3

FALTERING STEPS

Greetings. When I got home from the hospital, I was reading the devotional book, *Jesus Calling*, and felt that the message was just for me that day. "My power flows most freely into weak ones aware of their need for Me. Faltering steps of dependence are not lack of faith; they are links to My Presence."[i]

This begins my journey back: **FALTERING STEPS** of dependence. Oh, do I know what that means now! At the doctor's orders we have begun walking around the neighborhood, five minutes at a time. I cannot believe how indescribably weak I am even though everyone told me I would be. You see, I had an arrogant confidence in my own strength. "Pick up your feet," my husband Fred keeps telling me, as we walk around the block. "Don't shuffle." I DO shuffle, though. My legs, especially as we near home, tremble and I am unable to lift my feet. It's more than I can do. So I lean on his arm. I'm shuffling but I make it. I think maybe shuffling and faltering steps of dependence are much the same thing. No strength, or not enough anyway, to lift the feet. It could be illness, recovery, pain, age or simply exhaustion.

So here I am with the reality of my helplessness gripping me. This is all I can do right now. The weakness in myself is difficult to absorb. But Christ's power rests upon me; is made perfect in my capitulation to Him. "And He said to me, 'My grace is sufficient for you, for my strength is made perfect in weakness.'" 2 Corinthians 12:9. Yes, I am shuffling. It's okay, because I'm leaning on Him, just as I need Fred's arm for our round-the-block forays.

God knows where I am right now. He knows how weak and needy I am, and asks me to come to Him with open hands ready to hold on to Him and an open heart to receive and know His strength. A long time ago I wrote the following and believe it also applies now:

INVITATION

"This is what the LORD says: 'Stand in the ways and see, and ask where the good way is, and walk in it, and you will find rest for your souls.'" Jeremiah 6:16

I seem to be standing immobile at a crossroad,
yearning to know the peace of the center of God's will.

My heart is crying, pleading for His direction.
Surely He will show me where He wants me,
so I listen, careful to discern His presence,
to hear the whisper in my soul.

Then He speaks, and in the very depths of me
I sense His arms outstretched in welcome.
His guiding voice, so tender, breathes,
"Come here."

It is an invitation that I long to accept with all that I am. And so this is the direction my faltering steps will take me. My body will grow stronger and my legs will once again have the ability to lift my feet. I do not however, want to forget what I am learning now, so I continue to be mindful of the necessity of dependence on Jesus, and that shuffling faltering leaning steps are what bring me closer to Him.

STANDING

Good Morning. I am hesitant about writing today. Today hasn't been very good. Since I am trying to be honest and forthright however about this recovery process, I'll try. They told me at the hospital there would be days like this; days I would feel down and blue. Of course I thought *I'd* never ever feel a mite depressed, because my normal tendency is to be upbeat and encouraging! But I was wrong. For the past couple of days I have been really low. I have not felt like doing anything even though I have tried to do *something* each day to lift myself up and mark a signpost on the journey.

Fortunately the days have been beautiful, and Fred encourages me to head out a couple of times a day to walk and build up my strength. The hospital staff has given me a pedometer so that I can count my steps, with a goal of 10,000 steps a day, which I will hopefully reach at some time in the future.

I was thinking that I might need a spiritual pedometer to measure my spiritual steps. I seem to be at a dead stop spiritually, still struggling to find an emotional reaction, to hear God speak to my heart. I feel so distant from that place of intimacy that I so desire. Perhaps instead of trying so hard to recapture it, I should simply immerse myself in the Word and let it happen.

As I was pondering a series of devotionals on faith the other day, I was reading about Moses in Exodus as the children of Israel stood on the shore of the raging Red Sea and the pursuing Egyptians behind them. "And Moses said to the people, 'Do not be afraid. Stand still, and see the salvation of the LORD, which He will accomplish for you today. The LORD will fight for you, and you shall hold your peace.'" Exodus 14:13a-14.

The writer of this devotional, Babbie Mason, says, "Often in an effort to encourage a person we offer the words 'It will be all right. You just hang in there.' But *hanging* paints a picture of dangling out of control, vulnerable and exposed. More to the point I choose to say, 'It will be all right. You just _stand_ in there.'"[ii]

Because we have a firm foundation upon which to stand confidently, we can be still and watch God work. That thought reached my heart. I think I can say that the second signpost on this road is **STANDING**; not allowing the down days to discourage me because, in truth I am standing on the promises. Remember the old hymn? "Standing on the promises of Christ my King; through eternal ages let his praises ring; glory in the highest, I will shout and sing, standing on the promises of God."[iii]

There, I guess I do feel better!

ARISE

What a week it has been! I will try to recapture some of the things that have marked it as special. I was able to sing with my friends at a lovely fashion show here in the community where we live. I wanted to attend so I asked our director if I could sing at the show if I came to rehearsal earlier that week. He said yes, so I went to rehearsal just long enough to get familiar with our song. On Friday I got dressed up and went to the fashion show. My very first *official* outing. I sang my heart out, and it was so much fun to see so many friends who had prayed and supported us through the past weeks. I enjoyed it but I was thoroughly exhausted after those two hours.

Then, on Saturday I had the distinct honor and privilege of presenting the eulogy for my dear friend Sharon at her celebration of life. She went to be with Jesus just about the time I came home from the hospital. What joy it was, yet what tears flowed as we remembered her and I was able to share what she had meant to me over the many years of our friendship. Again, after the emotion and travel of that day, exhaustion didn't begin to describe how I felt. So, once more, I had to acknowledge the weakness and lack of strength and stamina in my body, even while bowing in gratitude to God for what He supplied.

Sunday I made it to church for the first time since the surgery and was heartened by the music and the message and the hugs of those who had carried me to the Throne of Grace with their prayers.

Now today I went back to my doctor for blood tests and an exam to see how I'm healing after a month of recuperation. He seemed to be thrilled at my status.

So what is my signpost for this week? What have I learned? How has God met me? What keeps repeating in my head is

ARISE. It's time to return to the land of "getting out of the recliner!" To put myself out there a bit and get back to the comfort and challenge of being part of the community of friends and family into which God has placed me. To begin to go with the flow of my life as much as I am physically able.

In my quiet time I have been reading about the children of Israel and their wilderness wanderings. In a way I feel as though I have been in a wilderness of sorts; my wandering called resting, healing. But as I read in the book of Joshua, I found these verses. God is speaking to Joshua after Moses has died. "Now therefore arise, go over this Jordan, you and all this people, to the land which I am giving to them—the children of Israel." Joshua 1:2. And in Joshua 1:6, the following encouraging words appear, "I will not leave you or forsake you. Be strong and of good courage." Oh how I rely on that promise.

It's time to arise, I guess. I feel God's hand on the small of my back, His voice in my ear. Just as He didn't push His children, but walked with them, so it is with me. Though He impels me with His command, His presence strengthens me and His word nourishes me. I think it is time to move!

WRAPPED

Greetings. Last week was full of emotion…excitement, sadness, joy, anticipation, dread, gratitude, affirmation. I can't help but look back and re-examine some of that, as arising has begun in earnest. Cardiac rehab started today, beginning the schedule that will be in effect for the next three months, three times a week, so I can embrace the conditioning of my body to get and stay healthy. I feel rebellious at the thought of all that time given up, but I realize the necessity of it, and will do it, even as I gripe, then feel guilty about griping. It really is a blessing that it is available to me.

My signpost today is **WRAPPED**. I am sensing God's arms wrapped securely about me; hearing Him whispering His love into my heart. I was struck by this as I was reading in Isaiah, chapter 12, "Your anger is turned away, and You comfort me. Behold, God is my salvation, I will trust and not be afraid; for YAH, the LORD, is my strength and song; He also has become my salvation." Isaiah 12:1b-2. The truth of that was made so real to me last week as I wrote and delivered the words to memorialize my friend. Though I was weak in the flesh and sad in heart, God's strength carried me, bringing to my soul a great gift. Amid the emotional turmoil He gave me peace and comforted me so I could offer comfort to others. "Blessed be the God and Father of our Lord Jesus Christ, the Father of mercies and God of all comfort, who comforts us in all our tribulation that we may be able to comfort those who are in any trouble, with the comfort with which we ourselves are comforted by God." 2 Corinthians 1:3-4.

Even though my head knew that God was holding me tightly, I haven't *felt* it before. He, the God of all comfort, wraps me in His mighty arms, and now I *know* it deep in my soul. I am exhilarated to contemplate the reality of it. My heart sings strong!

PRAISE

I am still seeking signposts along the road to recovery. My signpost for this week is **PRAISE**. Whatever comes, whatever is going on…praise God. He desires us, even commands us, to give Him praise. In the Old Testament, chiefly in the Psalms, there are so many instructions to praise Him. In fact Psalm 150:6 says, "Let everything that has breath praise the LORD. Praise the LORD!" And in the New Testament in Hebrews 13:15, "Therefore by Him let us continually offer the sacrifice of praise to God, that is, the fruit of our lips, giving thanks to His name." I'm seeing afresh that sometimes praise *is* a sacrifice. I don't always feel like praising Him. Yet it cannot be stressed strongly enough that God longs for praise from His people.

I have been praising Him for what He has done by way of healing; for the many visible, tangible ways I have seen Him work. My very life is a testament to His preserving. Fred says that every time he sees my incisions, he is filled with praise for my life. When I see the scars I just think how ugly they are. I have yet to fully comprehend how close I came to not being here. So yes, I have praised God for that. But honestly there is still an angry part of me; angry that everything has changed. I wonder what is ahead for me. Can I truly praise when I feel stopped in my tracks? That's where the sacrifice comes in. To lay it all on the altar of praise, trusting Him for the next step, the next signpost.

So it brought me to tears when I heard the lyrics to the song, "Broken Hallelujah," performed by a group called The Afters. So many times melodies and lyrics touch my poet's heart and I completely identified with these lyrics. "Even though I don't know what your plan is, I know You're making beauty from these ashes."[iv]

It is written from a place of pain, I believe, and even though the writer feels barely able to stand, and prayer seems difficult, we are told to praise God anyway. That is kind of how I feel right now. I don't understand. But God hears my heart. I guess the truth is that we don't need to see exactly what God is doing in order to praise Him. The song goes on to say, "I've seen joy and I've seen pain. On my knees I call Your name. Here's my broken Hallelujah."v

My dear friends, from the depths of my heart I encourage you to lift a song of praise to our God, whatever is in your life right now, and sing with me as I raise my hands in my own obedient, although broken, Hallelujah!

EXERCISE

"Faith is believing that God will make good on what He has said; and the faith is in the place of what you ask, until what you ask is yours."[vi] You might have to pause and read that a couple of times. I have. I've been doing some studying on faith lately and I found that quote by Vonette Bright, the wife of the founder of Campus Crusade for Christ, and it intrigues me.

My signpost for the week is the subject that has been dominating my activities lately...**EXERCISE**.

As part of my healing, the doctor prescribed cardiac rehab. Three times a week I descend into the lower regions of St. Peter's Hospital for an hour and a half of a designed regimen of walking, biking and weights. I am committed to this for three months, and I have to tell you, I do not like exercise. Never have, which probably contributed to the heart issues! Thus in order to regain my strength and stamina and avoid further problems, I'm doing it. It's hard work, but I'm finding faith is hard work too. Faith grows by exercising it. I'd like to quote a few more wise words from Vonette Bright. "Your faith will grow as you personally experience His faithfulness to fulfill His promises. Start small and exercise believing just like you exercise your body — little by little until you can do more."[vii]

I started very small at rehab...one pound weights, five minute bursts of walking. Today, just a few weeks later, I did thirty minutes on the bike and used three-pound weights.

Amazingly, my body is stronger. It takes a large chunk of time out of my days, and truthfully, I'd much rather be home in my recliner!

However, I'm discovering I have to put my *rather* to rest and head out to the gym if I want to please my doctor and get well. I have to dust off my sagging faith and really believe in God's promises if I want to please Him and find healing for my soul. Because, as we are told in Hebrews 11:6, "But without faith it is impossible to please Him, for he who comes to God must believe that He is, and that He is a rewarder of those who diligently seek Him."

Diligence. **EXERCISE**. Great signposts for anyone's journey.

GRIEF

Greetings. I have been struggling with something unfamiliar to me this week. I have discovered **GRIEF.** I hate to admit it, which means further that I am in the denial stage. The other day at my rehab class they showed a video that describes the relational, emotional part of having heart surgery. That video completely affirmed and validated what I have been feeling. As my emotions have begun to wake up, I am finding a deep grieving for what was my "before."

They told me that the surgery would make my heart as good as new, and so I had the mistaken belief that I was cured. Now I am learning that I still have heart disease, and as my son the nurse pointed out, *serious* heart disease. This rocks me. I don't even want to say that, nor do I want to say "I have diabetes." It means that my health is forever compromised, and for the rest of my life, I will have to watch what I do, what I eat, how I respond. I am grieving the freedom I felt, before, of blithely flying through my days without a care for those things. It makes me angry somehow.

I realize that for many of my readers this process is a familiar one. Perhaps you are going through something like this yourself. However, it is new to me. *Grief.* I have not experienced it very often in my life and I am grateful for that. Yes, I lost my parents when I was young, and there have been other sad things happen. But this is new and different somehow.

Most of us know there are stages of grief: denial, anger, bargaining, depression, acceptance. We can go back and forth between them and they don't always follow the same pattern, but we will go through them all. I've said before that I did not think I would experience this grief the doctors and nurses described, especially considering my childhood losses, the epitome of grieving, enough to last for a lifetime. But how wrong I was!

So here I am with a heavy heart. I don't want to make light of what I am feeling, so I am trying to describe it and come to terms with what it means to me. Grief is a reaction to loss. Had there been nothing wonderful to celebrate previously, there would be no grief. The mourning is part of the process of saying goodbye to something beloved, and it comes to us all. Whether it is the loss of a loved one, loss of health, loss of freedom in any way, it can be a bitter pill. In my struggle, I am reminded of a very favorite verse in Isaiah 53:4a. "Surely, He has borne our griefs and carried our sorrows," speaking of Jesus willingly going to the cross for us and I am comforted. All the griefs of the world were borne on the shoulders of my Savior. My grief, your grief, included. And He invites us to lean on those shoulders as well.

Grief has poured over me this week and I have finally recognized it, acknowledged it for what it is. I have also discovered that there is one positive thing. For many years my heart had been sealed against the hurt over my son who was out of my life until this heart incident.

As my feeling is returning, I find myself absolutely overwhelmed with love for him to the point of tears. Yes, tears. Finally my son is back! I cannot hold him tightly enough and I burst with joy to hear him speak love to me. Now, even as grief grips me, I can still find joy in the reopening of my heart, having my family restored. A paradox indeed, grief and joy intermingled. I was grateful with my head that this has happened, but now it is real in my heart.

As for the grief, considering the path that still lies ahead, I say with the Psalmist, "I wait for the LORD, my soul waits, and in His word I do hope. My soul waits for the Lord more than those who watch for the morning—yes, more that those who watch for the morning." Psalm 130:5-6.

Knowing I am held in the palm of God's hand, and that He is working in me, I welcome the process of working through the mourning, watching for the morning, confident that He is already there.

CHOICE

Good Morning. Deuteronomy 30:19-20 says, "I call heaven and earth as witnesses today against you, that I have set before you life and death, blessing and cursing; therefore choose life, that both you and your descendants may live; that you may love the LORD your God, that you may obey His voice, and that you may cling to Him, for He is your life and the length of your days..."

It's a great day today! Summer is here and spirits lift with the beauty that surrounds us. The beauty of the Word of God has captured my heart this week, and as you can no doubt see from the verses I quoted above, my signpost for this week is **CHOICE**.

Choices govern our lives every moment. And I am realizing that as I proceed with my recovery, the matter of making choices is very near to me. I don't like to go to the rehab center and exercise for an hour three times a week, or walk for thirty minutes around the neighborhood, but I am choosing to do it because if I don't, the chances of healing grow slimmer.

As I've said previously, I don't like to admit that I have heart disease, but I am choosing to say it until I believe it. If I do not, the reality will fade, and I will stay in denial and not take care of the things that will help me. I so want a glazed doughnut, but every day I drive past the bakery without stopping. It's my choice. How many times have I heard a young parent say to a child, "You have to learn to make better choices." I sort of feel like that child, hearing my heavenly Father say it to me. A long time ago I wrote a little meditation on the verses I quoted, and I've included it here.

THE CHOICE
Would you have blessing?
Choose life.
Would you be fruitful?

Choose God.
Would you dwell peacefully in your land?
Choose life
Would you have protection?
Choose God.
Would you have a new spirit?
Choose life.
Would you have a new heart?
Choose God.
Today God calls heaven and earth to record
that He sets before you
life and death, blessing and cursing.
Choose Him, for He is your life.
O Child of God, how could you choose
the other way!

These Deuteronomy verses have called out to me, highlighting my weekly signpost. There is now another choice I must make: to trust God implicitly. And so I choose to love Him, obey and cling to Him, because He is my life and the length of my days. Hallelujah!

I have no idea what my next signpost will be, because I'm only taking it one step, one **CHOICE**, at a time.

ALIVE

Greetings. I found my signpost in neon this week. But first a little history…some time ago I read author Debbie Macomber's book, *One Perfect Word*.[viii] In it she advocates choosing a word for the year, and shares how she has done this for years; praying and asking God to show her the "word" that He wishes to use in her life in the coming year. As a word person I found that fascinating, and have tried it myself a couple of times. As this year began, I was moved when I read Romans 6:11, "Likewise you also, reckon yourselves to be dead indeed to sin, but alive to God in Christ Jesus our Lord." My word for this year is **ALIVE**. I wrote in my journal at the beginning of the year, "It will be interesting to see how it plays out in my life. What will I learn if I focus on that life I have available in me as a believer in Jesus?"

Such a deep thought! However, in all of the hullabaloo surrounding the heart incident and subsequent surgery, I had totally forgotten about my one perfect word. Now this week, months later, as I was paging back through my journal I saw it as plain as day. **ALIVE**. And an overwhelming joy swept over me in the fact that I am alive! That even as God directed my choice of a word for this year, He was going to let me know just how incredible that is. My body is waking up. The numbness surrounding my chest and arm incisions is going away. Healing is taking place there. My spirit is waking up. The numbness surrounding my emotions is decreasing and I find myself able once again to feel.

My soul is waking up. The numbness surrounding my relationship with God is disappearing and I find a quiet delight in the truth that I am alive to God in Christ Jesus. My scars are a reminder that I have been given new life, and even as I rejoice, I am quickly drawn to the redemption and restoration that God has given me: new, radiant life. **ALIVE** in every way.

No wonder my heart is singing with the psalmist: "Bless the LORD, O my soul, and all that is within me, bless His holy name! Bless the LORD, O my soul, and forget not all His benefits; who forgives all your iniquities, who heals all your diseases, who redeems your life from destruction, who crowns you with lovingkindness and tender mercies, who satisfies your mouth with good things, so that your youth is renewed like the eagle's." Psalm 103:1-4.

Thanks for walking this journey with me.

CARE

Often I find myself not knowing what to write. Today I've tossed aside several ideas that just didn't seem right, and I thought I might have to miss this week because nothing was working in my thinking processes.

But then I had occasion to visit a friend in the hospital after I finished my cardio rehab session. As I walked down the hall, everything was very familiar. Different floor, but the same atmosphere as when I was there just three months ago. It took me back, I can tell you. What struck me was how much I had depended on my husband during those days; how I waited until he entered my room to make everything okay. So I've decided it's time to pay tribute to him and all he did for me. My signpost for this week is **CARE**.

He came every day and usually spent all day and evening with me. And even when I was sleeping (which was most of the time) he remained steadfast. Feeling his care for me in such a tangible way, I was blessed indeed! Thank God for Fred.

That care never diminished when I got home--in fact, it increased. He was vigilant with my medications, measuring each dose and making sure I took them. He watched over me, alert for any sign of pain or discomfort and was so sympathetic and helpful. He even rigged a frame to keep the blankets off my feet so I could sleep comfortably on my back. He cooked, made smoothies, heated soup, made incredible chili and dedicated every moment of his time to me. I so loved his undemanding attention to my every need--even helping me shower, until I could do it myself. Of course, since I am recovering so well, the necessity of a shower assist has pretty much ended. But I have the sweet memory of being cherished in my really dire need, and I appreciate him so very much more than I ever had before.

This is how God desires to care for us. I see that so plainly now. The man He gave me for a life's companion reflected God's devotion to my needs. Just as I depended on the loving care of my husband, my Heavenly Father waits for me to, as he instructs in 1 Peter 5:6-7, "Therefore humble yourselves under the mighty hand of God, that He may exalt you in due time, casting all your care upon Him, for He cares for you."

I prayed, "God, thank You for showing me in such a precious way Your **CARE** for me. And thank You for my husband. I am so grateful."

MUSIC

Greetings! "Whenever I am afraid, I will trust in You. In God (I will praise His word), in God I have put my trust; I will not fear. What can flesh do to me?" Psalm 56:3-4.

I woke up afraid this morning. Yesterday the doctor called with my latest blood test results and announced that there was a problem with my kidneys, and I needed to come back in and discuss it. I felt sick. He also said my diabetes wasn't under control. It seemed a big bump in the road and I imagined all sorts of scenarios. Fortunately I was able to get in to see him right away.

But back to the fear...I thought I wouldn't be able to sleep last night, but I did and awoke with the above verse running through my head. What comfort! My spirit calmed and I headed for my rehab session. I put a favorite CD in the player and let the music and lyrics roll over me to penetrate the fear and send it packing. The first song was Bryan Duncan's "When I Turn to You."[ix]

It's a prayer, really, demonstrating a deep realization that when we turn to God, He is always waiting, always watching, with an understanding heart and eyes that see beyond anything we can see. And we learn what really matters: that He is always merciful and that we are forgiven. He ends the song with this tender chorus: "I no longer look for a place to hide 'cause I know where I belong. When I turn to you I know that I love you."[x]

It turns out that the kidney issue is not as serious as I had feared--a bit of tweaking of medications should take care of it. But I am rejoicing, not only for that, but for the way God ministered to me this morning, both with His word, and with music that touched me. Though I am feeling somewhat more fragile and vulnerable than I was, I turned to my loving Father and found His strength, His comfort and His love, whatever happens. No more need to cower in fear and apprehension, because I know where I belong--under the shelter of His care. It is pure joy, and I really hope I remember this day when the enemy once again tries to trap me. In light of that, I think my signpost for the week might be **MUSIC**. What do you think? Because that's what I found in Him this morning, the music of His promises.

After a really tough weekend, crying with friends who lost someone precious and spending time with other friends who are facing the final separation from their loved one, (whom we also love), the peace of God's love is near and precious in spite of a little fear detour. I am trusting that you are experiencing what He so freely offers.

REFRESHMENT

Good Morning. Welcome to my meandering heart. My signpost for the week is **REFRESHMENT.** It has been a sweet recurring theme in my reading of scripture, and is soothing to my soul.

We are grieving the loss of a dear friend. And suffering as well with other friends who are grieving. At times it can seem too much to bear, as though we are in a desert of loss and heartache. But it is comforting to find so many passages where God turns the wilderness into pools of water, and streams in the desert. It certainly has refreshed me.

I have been asked to read scripture at our friend's memorial celebration. In searching for the best passage to read, I came across Psalm 107, and I have been living in it for days. Here is a snippet of refreshment for all of us. "He turns a wilderness into pools of water, and dry land into watersprings. There He makes the hungry dwell, that they may establish a city for a dwelling place, and sow fields and plant vineyards, that they may yield a fruitful harvest." Psalm 107:35-37.

While the truth of God's refreshing is comforting, I am also discovering that it has a purpose. For the children of Israel it was to build a city, plant and harvest, to regain what they had lost through their rebellion. For us, it's that we strengthen our resolve to sow seeds of His word, plant kindness and service that we will be fruitful.

I am refreshed in the midst of desert sadness, but I must not let it rest there. May I be compelled to share, plant and take His comfort wherever I go. Are you in need of comfort? He stands ready to refresh you. Seek Him in His word.

FREEDOM

Greetings! I hope your summer is all that you hoped it would be. It is going by swiftly with beautiful warm days and lots of sunshine. Of course, there are weather tragedies and terrible things happening all over our country this summer and our hearts go out to those dear folks who have lost so much.

It's been a bittersweet week for me. Saying goodbye to a dear friend at a wonderful memorial service on Friday was a day filled with emotion. Sadness, yet joy as well for us, because during the service we had our sons with us to remember the years that we celebrated and we found solace in the memories. It was so good for all of us to be together.

So, do I have a signpost for this week? It's been confusing, in a sense, fluctuating between feeling down in the dumps and feeling hopeful. But yesterday morning during my time with God, I received a sweet signpost from His word that I want to share with you. It is **FREEDOM**. I've been dancing around it, I think, during this recovery time, using words that might seem to have the same meaning, but I really heard a new take on this word as I studied John 8:31-32. How often we have heard this, "You shall know the truth, and the truth shall make you free." It sounds like a great plan.

But I'm thinking that you can't separate the two verses... Jesus says in Verse 31, "If you abide in My word, you are My disciples indeed." Verse 32 follows: "And you shall know the truth and the truth shall make you free." It's the *if/then* connection that grabbed me. The truth that can set us free comes from abiding in His word, from comprehending and absorbing it, walking in obedience. From what can it set us free?

Well for me the truth is that God loves me no matter what. I need to know freedom from the bondage of thinking that I have to perform. Freedom to let go of my own desires. Freedom from the tyranny of the clock. Freedom to let God love me, instead of stiff-arming His lavish love until I have done what I think I should do to earn it.

I know this is not a new concept, but it strikes my heart afresh with an arrow of just how true this freedom can be. Now that I can't do a lot of the things I used to feel were so important, the freedom not to feel guilty is beautiful. My freedom comes from His word; abiding in it, living in it, memorizing it, soaking in it. That brings true liberty. And I am grateful.

My prayer for you is that if you have not truly experienced His truth and freedom that you will dig into His word, without which it cannot be found. Be blessed by it this week.

FRUIT

Hello Friends. There are times I find it more difficult to write, because there are so many things I want to share, so many lessons I'm learning from the Word of God in my early morning quiet times. Maybe I should just say "morning" because it's not always early. I long for uninterrupted time to spend at the computer, but it seems there are so many distractions. Like the cardiac rehab for example. While I am very grateful for it, it saps me of so many hours of time and energy. I have nine more sessions at the hospital and then I will form a plan that I can do here at home and at the fitness center and pool. Then perhaps I will have a more satisfying schedule. Hopefully that will help!

All that being said, my signpost for this week is **FRUIT.** I've been looking at the subject of liberty for the past few weeks, finding passages that deal with the freedom we have in Christ. This week I have been blessed by Galatians 5:22-23. "But the fruit of the Spirit is love, joy, peace, longsuffering, kindness, goodness, faithfulness, gentleness, self-control. Against such there is no law."

Such a familiar passage! However, as I looked closer and tried to find how it applied to my own life, I notice the word "fruit." Food…never far from my mind, as I am struggling to eat healthier. Soon I was ruminating about the word diet, and the contrast between a restrictive diet and a balanced diet. On the first kind of diet I'm hungry, angry at being told what to eat and what not to eat. I get irritated and cranky. Deprived. But on the second kind of diet, I feel healthy and able to have some control; control to make my own choices, free to eat what I want and pleased with myself when I don't want to eat (what I'm learning are) unhealthy things.

Which brings up another contrast to my mind…the one

between legalism and grace. When told constantly "thou shalt not," as I have been most of my life, I'm miserable, rebellious and wanting to do the forbidden. When I appropriate God's grace, it totally turns around and I usually make the right choices because I can. I choose.

Again it's so much like my life right now. I didn't want to do the cardiac rehab and I fought it because "everyone" said I had to. I went under protest and with a chip on my shoulder. Now, though, having learned so much from this opportunity I am joyfully participating. I am so much stronger, and delighted with myself for hanging in. I *want* to exercise because I'm experiencing such great results and I fully accept the necessity of making good choices. God has taught me much, and I am so very grateful. I'm discovering the joy of being yielded--and free! They *can* go hand-in-hand. Soon I will be done with the forced rehab, and we will see how willing I am to continue.

I trust that this will be the new Lois. Anyone want to go for a walk? It can be fruitful!

FOCUS

Greetings. Kind of overcast today. We've sort of become used to beautiful sunshiny skies every morning lately, but there is beauty in change and I like the silvery sky sometimes.

This is a strange week. Last time I wrote about fruit, and how it made me think about food, which is so often on my mind! But this week, food is *really* on my mind. We have four potlucks, company for dinner twice, a 50th anniversary party, a birthday party and a luncheon to look forward to this week. So it's no surprise that I'm giving serious consideration to the subject of *food*. I am grateful for the sweetness of fellowship with friends that takes place in each of these events. I want to make that perfectly clear. However, I am in need of controlling my food intake and everyone knows how difficult that is with potlucks and birthday cake.

I was in need of God's wisdom and comfort as my Bible fell open to the Psalms, particularly 141-143, some of my favorites. It was no accident. On Monday as I contemplated the past weekend and the week ahead, I began using the Psalmist's words to entreat my heavenly Father. "LORD, I cry out to You; make haste to me! Give ear to my voice when I cry out to You. Let my prayer be set before You as incense, the lifting up of my hands as the evening sacrifice." Psalm 141:1-2.

I read on. The next verse I have always thought referred to things I might say, "Set a guard, O LORD, over my mouth; keep watch over the door of my lips." Psalm 141:3. But suddenly it was a light turning on in my brain. Couldn't it also mean to guard against the things I might eat that are not good for me, delicious as they might be? It was a direct hit. I think both applications work: they both refer to enemies and the traps they set. I have an enemy: my appetite for sweets, and it can destroy all the work I have done to get healthy.

God almost spoke out loud in this verse, but I found an answer in Psalm 141:8. "But my eyes are upon You, O God, the LORD, in You I take refuge; do not leave my soul destitute."

I also found my weekly signpost here. **FOCUS:** The answer to so many of life's situations. My prayer is that I focus my eyes on God the Lord for the week ahead as I will be tempted in many ways--already have been. But I can also say confidently that He has reminded me with every serving to keep a watch over what enters my mouth. In many ways it's as important as what comes out of it. I was so blessed by finding these verses that spoke to my need. Let's all examine where our **FOCUS** lies. It can be a game-changer!

SADNESS

I am sad this week. Early on Monday morning, my brother Jim passed away. He is number three in the birth order of our family and I am number one. His health has not been good for a long time, as he was suffering from diabetes, which affected so many other aspects of his quality of life. He was first diagnosed when he was 19 and has been on insulin since then--nearly 50 years. Eight years ago he got very sick and ended up in a diabetic coma, and as a result, had lost his sight and his short-term memory. His wife has cared for him sacrificially and tenderly, but the truth is, she was worn out completely. There is some relief in the sadness, because he no longer suffers. Still, he is the first of the nine of us to go, and there is a tearing in the fragile fabric of my family. We will be heading for his memorial celebration in Montana in a couple of weeks, with as many of the siblings as are able to be there. I will be coveting your prayers. It's going to be difficult in many ways. And I am dealing with **SADNESS**.

On the up side, however, the results from my latest blood test indicate that my kidney function has returned to normal and all my numbers are good. The doctor said he is very pleased and couldn't ask for better results. I am praising God, and happy that I seem to be doing the right things. There are only three sessions left in my cardiac rehab program, and then I will be on my own, to continue to exercise for the rest of my life. I am so grateful to be living where we have a complete gym and swimming pool. That will make it easier.

There are a lot of things going on this month--our concert will be held soon. Health issues notwithstanding, I am so grateful that I have been able to continue as part of our community chorus. I'm helping with a women's retreat taking place at the end of the month which means there are several planning events scheduled for us to get ready for the retreat. I look at the month and wonder how I'm going to get it all done, feeling conflicted and over-whelmed. Then add into the mix an unplanned trip to Montana. I need your prayers, my faithful friends.

Pondering, I was reading in Psalms this morning, and found these uplifting verses: "Because You have been my help, therefore in the shadow of Your wings I will rejoice. My soul follows close behind You; Your right hand upholds me." Psalm 63:7-8. Even though my heart is sad, there is rejoicing possible when we rest under the shelter of God's wings. That strong right hand that upholds in both sorrow and joy brings comfort in the midst of suffering.

And I read the following statement from *Jesus Calling:* "Even the most confusing day opens up before you as you go step by step with Me. My Presence goes with you wherever you go, providing Light for your path."[xi]

I needed this today. Maybe you do, too. It is such a great comfort. I pray you are sensing His presence wherever you go.

REHEARSAL

"Rejoice in the LORD; O you righteous! For praise from the upright is beautiful. Praise the LORD with the harp, make melody to Him with an instrument of ten strings. Sing to Him a new song; play skillfully with a shout of joy." Psalm 33:1-3

I am glad to be able to sit for a few minutes this morning in the midst of so much activity, and concentrate on what God would have me write this week. Searching for a signpost, the only word that pops into my head is **REHEARSAL.** It seems that this is what is consuming my thoughts and time. The community chorus' big Fall Concert is rapidly approaching and not only are our practices more and more intense, there are more and more of them. We have worked very hard to make this event pleasing to our audiences, as well as to ourselves.

Practice, practice, practice. Over and over again. We have technical rehearsals, sectional rehearsals, a dress rehearsal, more rehearsals, and then, OPENING NIGHT!

This reminds me of a quote I heard Christian speaker Sheila Walsh say at a Women of Faith conference. She was talking about our lives on earth and the struggles that mark our existence here. She said, and I've never forgotten it, "This is our dress rehearsal, the warm-up of the orchestra, before the curtain opens wide and the real symphony begins."

As I ponder this, I find so many parallels between what we are experiencing right now and the truth of the real symphony Sheila describes. Just as we in our concert choir are anxious for opening night, for the believer there is a beautiful sense of anticipation for the curtain parting, so to speak, and eternity beginning.

All the memory of hard work, the practices and details, for those who belong to God, will be forgotten in the thrill of the eternal overture's opening chords--just as the applause and appreciation of the crowd dims the memory of all the hours of rehearsal.

In a very real sense, living for Jesus here on earth is practicing for eternity. We have a Director who leads us, a score to follow, companions who bring music and harmony to our paths. There is a sense of community and shared joy that only can be reached when all have the same goal. We all fail and have to repeat some of the measures of music over and over, but the end result is an opening night that transcends all expectation.

As I stand beneath the lights of the Opening Night of our concert, I pray I am also prepared for the really, really Big Show: the day when Heaven opens and my Savior appears to bring me home! Then all the practicing will be fulfilled in a new song and revealed in pure joy.

"But as it is written, 'Eye has not seen, nor ear heard, nor have entered into the heart of man the things which God has prepared for those who love Him.'" 1 Corinthians 2:9.

ANNIVERSARY

Good Morning! It's a good day. Dress rehearsal for our concert this weekend. All the work and practice will be paying off. I'm only giving it a passing glance in my meditation this week, however, because today is special in another way: our 49th **ANNIVERSARY**! And I am celebrating in my heart, lifting my praise to God for gifting me with Fred, my husband. This is where all my attention will be today.

I will also depart from my usual commentary to post something I wrote for him years ago. For me it describes what I feel for him. I trust you will enjoy it, and help us celebrate all those years. I am so very blessed.

UMBRELLA
"His banner over me is love." Song of Solomon 2:4

Walking along the beach at midnight,
the ocean gently laps the sand beneath my feet,
a cool breeze scents the air; I pause.

Sleep eludes me and the moon
has called me from our rumpled bed.
It's not restlessness I feel, not now,
but a longing to express my joy.

Silver streaks caress the surface,
rolling gently with the tide.
I reflect upon our life; the years spent side by side;
as moments ago I lay in your arms,
thanking God for the comfort He provides
for me by giving me you.

We are no longer young. Yet how gloriously sweet,
as heads turn gray and skin once firm begins to droop,
to feel the tingle of excitement, knowing that back there
you are tossing, turning, reaching out for me.

By the time my middle years arrived,
I thought I'd settle into the humdrum;
to create a groove through which my life would smoothly glide.
Peaks and valleys would subside,
and I would move between the boundaries like the sea.
I did not expect this thrill each day;
the fluttering expectance, the delight of being together.
I thought it would fade; this completeness
of joining heart, mind and body before God.

Now I know that love is contentment
and sharing mixed with flashes of joy.
As moonlight polishes the sea,
the patina of time together
brings a lightness of heart that comes
from releasing my burden
to the umbrella of your care.

My heart is full as I think of what God has given. Not only
the umbrella of Fred's care, but God's sovereign presence as well.
I praise Him.

AFTERWARD

Greetings. We are getting ready to head to Montana for my brother's memorial and would appreciate your prayers as we go.

But first, I want to share my signpost for this week with you. It is **AFTERWARD**. Does that sound strange? Did I mention that I have completed my cardiac rehab sessions--graduated, in a sense? And now it is incumbent upon me to go on with the exercise regimen recommended for me. I wonder if I have the discipline and strength to make the necessary choices that I am considering. As I ponder, I find myself going to a dear favorite Psalm.

I will quote some of the precious verses here: "You hold me by my right hand. You will guide me with Your counsel and afterward receive me to glory. Whom have I in heaven but You? And there is none upon earth that I desire besides You. My flesh and my heart fail; but God is the strength of my heart and my portion forever." Psalm 73:24-26.

Oh, there is such comfort in knowing that God holds me and will guide me. He is the strength that will enable me to make choices that will grant me continued health. I realize that this discipline must happen, and I will lean on the facts spoken in these verses for the rest of my life--I *have* to.

This reminds me of a quote attributed to Winston Churchill: "This is not the end. This is not, even, the beginning of the end. But it may, just possibly, be the end of the beginning."[xii] Interesting, isn't it? It's how I feel. You may have to read it more than once. I did.

My **AFTERWARD**, after the beginning of the change in my life with my heart issue, depends on me depending on God until He calls me home. As I trudge weary miles on the treadmill, I hope I keep my focus on Him and His plan for the rest of my life, and gladly perform the routine that includes swimming and biking and weight-lifting as well. I am grateful for the new, repaired heart, both my physical heart and the spiritual heart that beats in a new rhythm of God's grace and love.

How I thank you all for your support and prayers. You all mean so much to me!

FAMILY

We just got home from Montana last night and I leave tomorrow morning for the women's retreat. As a member of the retreat team I have to be there a day early to help get everything ready. So today is IT. Much to do, as you can imagine.

To report on our Montana trip...first of all, thank you for your prayers. All went well: God's protection on the roads, His gracious working out of all details, concluding with a tribute to my brother Jim. Very emotional and draining, but good. Losing him has cut a wide swath across what has been and what will be.

This week my word is **FAMILY**. Perhaps not a real signpost, but it's what has been so much in my thoughts and activities. My brothers and sisters and I are spread all over the country and don't get together very often, and when we do, there always seems to be a re-hashing of all that has gone wrong; some of the bad memories outweigh the good ones and we sort of get bogged down in "why we are the way we are."

As I sat down with my Bible this morning, asking God to speak to my heart, I opened to Isaiah 43. There is so much in this chapter that touches me and reminds me who I am in Him-- created, formed, made, redeemed, precious, honored, loved, preserved--it has been so instrumental in my healing process. But today I noticed a new application to my life in Isaiah 43:18-21: "Do not remember the former things, nor consider the things of old. Behold, I will do a new thing, now it shall spring forth; shall you not know it? I will even make a road in the wilderness and rivers in the desert. I give waters in the wilderness and rivers in the desert, to give drink to My people, My chosen. This people I have formed for Myself; they shall declare My praise."

There must come a time when we stop going back and giving such weight to the memories that keep *picking the scab*. I confessed to Fred that I am tired of going over and over what was wrong in our family. There were bad things, I'll be the first one to admit it; but there is this, as Jeremiah put it in the famous passage, "'For I know the thoughts that I think toward you,' says the LORD, 'thoughts of peace and not of evil, to give you a future and a hope.'" Jeremiah 29:11. I want to focus on NOW.

As I quickly recover from the surgery and wonder what is ahead, I cling to Isaiah 43:19 above and look forward to the new thing He will be doing in my life. I have no idea what is coming but I trust the One Who formed me for His purpose. In Isaiah 43:10-11, He states very clearly what that is: "'You are My witnesses,' says the LORD, 'and My servant whom I have chosen, that you may know and believe Me, and understand that I am He. Before Me there was no God formed, nor shall there be after Me. I, even I, am the LORD, and besides Me there is no savior.'"

There is a freshening in my spirit, water in the desert, an anticipation of the road ahead and a longing to know my God and draw all whom He places in my circle of influence, my **FAMILY**, to declare His praise!

SEVENTY

Greetings. I am feeling somewhat revived this morning. I got home from the women's retreat Sunday afternoon, exhausted yet knowing the joy and thrill of a mountaintop experience. The retreat was amazing and I was blessed beyond belief by our speaker Carol Kent and the time I was able to spend with her. I praise God for the encouragement she offered and the joy she spread all over the camp. However, after every mountaintop the valley looms and reality inserts itself. In my case reality means the weariness of the past three weeks catching up with me. I've slept every available moment. Perhaps I am not as fully recovered from the surgery as I would like to think.

In any case, I am happy to be able to share some thoughts with you this morning. I was reading in Numbers the story of the children of Israel complaining that they had only manna to eat and they were making Moses' life miserable. He then cries out to God, "Why have You afflicted Your servant? And why have I not found favor in Your sight, that You have laid the burden of all these people on me? Did I conceive all these people? Did I beget them, that You should say to me, 'Carry them in your bosom, as a guardian carries a nursing child,' to the land which You swore to their fathers? Where am I to get meat to give to all these people? For they weep all over me, saying, 'Give us meat, that we may eat.' I am not able to bear all these people alone, because the burden is too heavy for me." Numbers 11:11-14.

I read that and thought to myself, "That sounds a lot like my whining." It's not the same burden, but the same spirit. "I am so tired, and there is so much to do," seems to be my mantra. But as I read further I found God's response to Moses was to have him pick seventy elders to come alongside him, and God would "take of the Spirit that is upon you and will put the same upon them;

45

and they shall bear the burden of the people with you, that you may not bear it yourself alone." Numbers 11:17.

This all came together for me last night when a precious friend whispered in my ear, "You are always in my prayers." It struck me that God has provided my *seventy* by bringing prayer support alongside upon which I can depend. As Jan Silvious says, "No one can mature and accomplish your life's purpose in a vacuum."[xiii] We need each other. I need your prayer support. You need mine. God never expects us to carry any burden alone. Not only does He supply His strength, but tangible support as well, with friends and family that come alongside to empower with their prayers. Are you part of someone's *seventy*? I feel strengthened today, knowing out there is my *seventy*, and I trust that I am part of a *seventy* for you, as God lays you upon my heart.

It may sound strange, but I think my signpost for this week is **SEVENTY**. And I am resting in that fact.

VALLEY

Good Morning. I trust all is well with you, as you pause to spend some time with me. I believe that this week my signpost is **VALLEY.** Mainly because that's where I think I am right now. The retreat last week was amazing, a really exciting, spiritual jolt! But then, there's the valley.

I talked last week a bit about my physical tiredness and I am recovering from that, but for some reason this week I have felt down and overwhelmed, which surprised me because I thought that once the retreat was finished I would feel great. But unfortunately I have been struggling against a sense of despair and sadness instead. The hospital and all the medical professionals warned us that this would happen at some point, but I figured since I was over five months out and still hadn't experienced any depression that I was home free. Fred thinks that it simply caught up with me, due to the fact that I was running from it so fast! He's probably right...

I confess that I am in a valley right now. Yet I know that my God waits for me here, and fills the valley with His loving Presence. A long time ago I wrote a poem called "Fountain in the Valley" based on Isaiah 41:17-18 "The poor and needy seek water, and there is none, their tongues fail for thirst. I the LORD will hear them, *I* the God of Israel will not forsake them. I will open rivers in desolate heights, and fountains in the midst of the valleys; I will make the wilderness a pool of water, and the dry land springs of water."

All this week the words in that meditation have been running through my head. I'm adding it today.

FOUNTAIN IN THE VALLEY
I stumble into the valley, soul-dry, thirsty,

choking on dust kicked up by rebellious heels,
my spirit a desert.
Mountain-top euphoria is a distant memory
to which I long to return,
but strength is needed for the climb
and I am dry.

Where is the delight? The joy?
Eclipsed by selfish goals, I turned my face from Yours
and I am dry.

Here in the valley a fountain waits,
a waterspout for my parched heart,
a pool in the wilderness to quench and cool.
The pages of Your Word are life-giving rivers.
I drink, and am no longer dry.

How these words that God poured out in my heart long ago comfort me; how they challenge and encourage me now today in another valley. I am thirsty, but I know that as soon as I open my Bible, the fountain will erupt and springs of living water will flow. He has promised, and He is faithful. Are you in your own **VALLEY** this week? I encourage you to find the precious refreshment of the living Word of God.

RESTORATION

We have been out of town on a tour speaking at a couple of luncheons, and we had been on the road before that, helping our son with his fund-raising golf tournament. Needless to say, I am TIRED!

My signpost for the week didn't happen until this morning. But it is a special one for me. **RESTORATION**. In my Bible reading I was at the 23rd Psalm, and I read it a little bit quickly, thinking "this is so familiar; what can God possibly say to me here?"

Listen. "The LORD is my shepherd; I shall not want. He makes me to lie down in green pastures; He leads me beside the still waters; He restores my soul; He leads me in the paths of righteousness for His name's sake." Psalm 23:1-3. These hauntingly lovely words jumped off the page: "the still waters" and "He restores my soul." How I have been longing for stillness in my life, for time just to BE. For rest and restoration, and to hear God's voice leading me. It was as though I heard Him say, "I *am* doing this for you. I love you and long to lead you. All you need to do is follow Me."

Peace settled over me, and as I read the words over and over again my soul was beginning the process of restoration. Feeling depleted by activities and responsibilities, I haven't allowed God's presence to fill me, resorting to trying in my own strength. No wonder I am tired!

A wonderful thing happened this morning. I realized I can still do the things I need and want to do as long as I stay wrapped in arms that hold me, stilling the roiling waters of my life and let my nourishment come from the green pastures of His Word. This is what soul restoration is all about. I am so grateful for God's promise to provide it.

I hope this makes sense to you. Maybe you need to be reminded of the wonder of being God's little lamb too, being led, sheltered and nourished as He gently restores your soul. It matters from *where* we venture out each day, and strength comes not from ourselves but straight from Him. What a realization. What a dose of truth!

LIGHT

Greetings! Hope all is well with you this afternoon. Believe it or not, we had some beautiful sunshine this morning and we were able to take a walk and get some fresh air. I know the rain will come back--it IS Washington, after all--but rainy days make the sunshine all the sweeter! Much the same as life, isn't it?

I have been writing about my struggle with feeling down and dispirited. That sense of discouragement still nips at my heels, but it is getting better. Praise God! When I prepare to share with you, I usually look back over the week in my journal to remind myself where God has touched my life, and today was no exception. I had been reading the other day in Psalm 139; that lovely passage that speaks of God's intimate knowledge of each one of us, how He has "fearfully and wonderfully made us," but as I was reading more of the psalm, what caught my eye were the words in Psalm 139:11- 12. "If I say, 'surely the darkness shall fall on me,' even the night shall be a light about me; indeed the darkness shall not hide from You, but the night shines as the day; the darkness and the light are both alike to You."

I guess that since I've been feeling darkness crowding at the edges of my emotions, this caught my eye; and I prayed, "Father even when I'm feeling a bit down, darkness may seem to be approaching, but I can reproach it, knowing that You surround me with light—the light of Your presence. 1 John 1:5 says, "God is light and in Him is no darkness at all." The darkness is a tool of my enemy and I have the choice of wrapping myself in it, or grabbing the covering of my God and repelling the darkness that threatens.

It sounds simple, and if I were *really* depressed, I would probably ask for help. But I realize it's an aftereffect of the surgery and it will pass. In the meantime, however, I have the wonder of the word of God, and meditating on it will be my medication. Because in Psalm 107:20 it says: "He sent His word and healed them."

I was thinking as I sat down to write this, of an analogy that makes sense to me. When I am in the swimming pool, I am buoyant--like I am moving gracefully and easily, held up by the water that surrounds me. That is not the case when I am walking on dry land! I am not graceful, nor do I move easily (pain in my hip and feet prevent that), and I said to myself. "Immersing myself in water is like allowing God's light to hold me up, filling me with His grace, and chasing away shadows of doubt and despair." I hope that makes sense to you...it surely does to me. With that, my signpost for this week is **LIGHT.** May I always choose to let the buoyancy of that light carry me.

And I will pray the same for each one of you!

STUBBORNNESS

I'm at it early this morning because I have a huge day ahead and need to get moving! Writing every week to you keeps me focused. Even though I journal every morning, it's still good to communicate outwardly, don't you think?

Speaking of focus, I'm not sure I am totally thrilled with my week. Let me explain. The world celebrated Halloween. We celebrated Harvest at our church, and I did help by handing out cookies at the party. Cookies in any way, shape or form are a danger to me. Even though we have never had a trick-or-treater here in the community where we live, we still buy a bag of candy *just in case*. What do we do with all the left over candy, you ask? Why, eat it, of course! And eat it, we did. All of it. We nibbled for a while grabbing one mini candy bar at a time, until the bag was half empty, then we simply sat and finished the whole thing. I can't believe I unwrapped one piece at a time, saying to myself, "You'll be sorry," but not letting that warning stop me. I did it anyway. And I WAS sorry. My stomach, long deprived of that kind of sweets, was not happy. Regretfully, my signpost this week is **STUBBORNNESS**.

But what occurred to me is that's how sin works in my life. Saying "no" to the flesh nature, and trying to walk in a God-pleasing manner by letting the Spirit help me control temptation works--it really does. For a while anyway, and then so often there will come a breakdown between God and me and I take a bite of something not so good. It tastes sweet for the moment and I indulge, knowing it's wrong, knowing I'll be sorry, yet doing it anyway.

That's just what I did with the candy bars, dropping wrapper after wrapper in the trash, stubbornly refusing to stop eating them. Considering this application, I am chagrined, yet

53

heartened by the fact of His limitless mercy and compassion for my weakness.

"The LORD is gracious and full of compassion, slow to anger and great in mercy. The LORD is good to all, and His tender mercies are over all His works." Psalm 145:8-9. Oh, thank You, God!

There is a song that has meant a lot to me in the past, and it surfaced in my mind this week. It is "Stubborn Love"[xiv] by Kathy Troccoli. On the day I really *heard* the words, I was driving down the road and had to pull over and weep with the truth of how God had loved me all through the years of my rebellion; how He drew me back. Some of her lyrics speak of God's love being stubborn and refusing to let go. These words ring in my heart. I hope they touch you. "And Your stubborn love, it never lets go of me. I don't understand how You can stay. Perfect love embracing the worst in me. How I long for Your stubborn love."[xv]

It is truly an amazing fact that God knows all about us, yet loves us and pursues us so that we can find that perfect love.

That's it for now. I repent of my stubborn candy gorging, relishing the truth of God's love for me anyway. Know that I'm back to salads, and trusting that you all know the beauty of God's stubborn love for you too.

SACRIFICE

Greetings on a crisp, sunny, cold November morning. I guess a storm is expected, but for now, we can revel in the beauty of creation preparing itself for winter. Veterans Day has passed. The sales are over until the next holiday and we have paid our respects and given our thanks to all who have served, and still serve, our country.

But I wonder if we really grasp the deep meaning of sacrifice, even as we say the word. Webster defines it. "Sacrifice: the act of giving up, destroying, permitting injury to, or forgoing something valued for the sake of something having a more pressing claim." We say it very lightly sometimes, I think, "Thank you for your sacrifice;" forgetting that the very act is a renouncing of something very precious for the greater good.

My signpost for the week, although it doesn't really pertain to my recovery, is **SACRIFICE**, because I want to be sure that I begin to comprehend what sacrifice means to someone in the military. I sort of understand because every time I waved Fred off to sea, there was a sacrifice being made. But ever so much more precious is to think of Jesus' willingness to give up everything for something that had a more pressing claim--us. His love for His broken world. A sacrifice can only be made by being willing to give up something of value. And He was willing.

Hear Philippians 2:9-11 from The Message: "Think of yourselves the way Christ Jesus thought of himself. He had equal status with God but didn't think so much of himself that he had to cling to the advantages of that status no matter what. Not at all. When the time came, he set aside the privileges of deity and took on the status of a slave, became human. Having become human, he stayed human. It was an incredibly humbling process. He didn't claim special privileges. Instead, he lived a selfless, obedient life and then died a selfless, obedient death, and the worst kind of death at that: a crucifixion. Because of obedience, God lifted him high and honored him far beyond anyone or anything, ever, so that all created beings in heaven and on earth-- even those long ago dead and buried--will bow in worship before this Jesus Christ, and call out in praise that he is the Master of all, to the glorious honor of God the Father."[xvi]

That, my friends, is a sacrifice, and we must never thank Him lightly. May we always stop and think of the weight of importance in the word **SACRIFICE** before it rolls glibly off our tongues. I am convicted and challenged this week. As I read tribute after tribute to Veterans, my heart swells in gratitude to my Savior, who willingly gave the ultimate sacrifice for me.

STRENGTH

Well it's a new day to praise God! We are blessed to be teen-tending our grandchildren. We can't say babysitting, or child care anymore, because our grandchildren are 16 and 13 and are very responsible to care for themselves. We are simply the loving adult presence while our son and daughter-in-law are having a much-needed rest. But it's great to be here and enjoying some precious time with these amazing kids. It's easy to find my signpost for the week--it is **STRENGTH**. Not mine, God's.

As I looked back over my journal this morning I found this word so many times that I felt I need to comment on it. I actually highlighted it whenever I found it written on my journal pages. Last week was a full one--four talks and a bazaar. As I have mentioned a time or two before in this book, I am still recovering, even though I don't like to think that I am not completely whole yet. Speaking at a luncheon and sharing with women is an amazingly and wonderful experience, but when the adrenalin rush departs, I am totally exhausted!

Friday I spent getting ready to attend a holiday bazaar, selling my books and cards. I was at the end of my strength, weak and trembling on my trip, but I have to tell you that God was my strength. Each time I looked into scripture, picking up my pen, I found myself staring at verse after verse declaring truths of God's ever-present strength. Here are a few: "The LORD is my light and my salvation; whom shall I fear? The LORD is the strength of my life; of whom shall I be afraid?" Psalm 27:1, "I can do all things through Christ who strengthens me." Philippians 4:13.

I so relied upon and rested in that strength, because my own was depleted. A reading in our church service Sunday brought my attention to these verses:

"May the LORD answer you in the day of trouble; may the

name of the God of Jacob defend you; may He send you help from the sanctuary, and strengthen you out of Zion." Psalm 20:1-2. Additionally, verse 6 speaks of the "saving strength of His right hand."

But the capstone was Psalm 27:14, very familiar, bringing comfort and encouragement to my weary body. "Wait on the LORD; be of good courage, and He shall strengthen your heart; wait, I say, on the LORD."

As I waited upon Him every morning this week I was infused with purpose and yes, strength. He blessed me with so much more affirmation and joy than I ever expected. I am so thankful, more than I could ever say. And thus I bring to you the same instruction as He gave me in His word. "Wait on the LORD." Oh how He loves to see us leaning upon Him.

May you all be heartened and strengthened in Him this week.

THANKSGIVING

Homeward bound. We've spent the week with our grandkids and had a wonderful time with them, but now are heading home to begin another month of activities and preparing for Christmas.

A few Thanksgiving thoughts before the actual day arrives: I have so much for which to be thankful this year. Specifically, for my very life! And while I'm at it, I want to say that I am thankful for *all* my life, not simply that it was spared by the heart surgery. Thankful that I am loved; thankful for family and friends; and for Jesus Who gave so much for me. I hope you all can relate. Here is my **THANKSGIVING** prayer. It is also my signpost. May God's blessing rest upon you on this holy day.

"Be anxious for nothing, but in everything by prayer and supplication, with thanksgiving, let your requests be made known to God; and the peace of God, which surpasses all understanding will guard your hearts and your minds through Christ Jesus." Philippians 4:6-7

Guard my heart, Father,
from all that would steal it.
Keep it Yours by the peace beyond understanding
promised to me through Jesus.
Because of His sacrifice, anxiety ceases;
trusting in Your hand to put together all the pieces.
I ask you this, with thanksgiving.

REBUILDING

I've had a lot of time to spend with God this week, truly resting and relaxing; and it has been sweet. Many times He has spoken to me through His word and I thought I would share one day's musings with you today. Perhaps you wonder each week what the signpost will be. So I will get to it right away: **REBUILDING.**

I've decided to use "hope" as my devotional theme for the next month, and the first passage I was directed to was Lamentations 3:22-24, such a familiar part of scripture. "Through the LORD's mercies we are not consumed, because His compassions fail not. They are new every morning; great is Your faithfulness. 'The LORD is my portion;' says my soul, 'therefore I hope in Him!'" You will be reading a lot about hope in my column over the next days. It's a precious concept.

I was reading some devotional thoughts relating to grief, as well as to joy and sorrow; how they are both a part of our life's experience here on earth. They referred to how Jerusalem was destroyed and then rebuilt, but rebuilt differently. It never looked the same. Likewise, on 9/11 there was great destruction in New York City. Though it is being rebuilt, it will never look the same as before. As I pondered these thoughts, it occurred to me that my life's ministry will be rebuilt, too, but it will never be the same; because *I* am not the same.

Since I am still in the process of recovery from my heart surgery, I have no idea of how the landscape of my life will look, but trusting my Heavenly Father that it will be pleasing to Him.

My hope is that through His unfailing compassion, I will rest in Him and be getting ready for the rebuilding foundation stones to be laid for what He is going to do.

I went to a familiar passage in Jeremiah that has challenged me many times. Often I wonder just what God is calling me to do. I'm sure many of us wonder the same thing. Some years ago I was present at a conference where the speaker assured us that our calling is to know God and then to make Him known. I consider that the call on each of our lives--to know God and to make Him known. How we do that is to use whatever gifts and talents He has given us.

Chapter 1 speaks of Jeremiah's call, or commission, and I'd like to share Jeremiah 1:9-10 here. "Then the LORD put forth His hand and touched my mouth, and the LORD said to me: 'Behold, I have put My words in your mouth. See, I have this day set you over the nations and over the kingdoms, to root out and to pull down, to destroy and to throw down, to build and to plant.'"

Often there has to be a pulling down in order for a rebuilding to take place. I questioned many times why I had to be shut down for a while, even while knowing deep inside that there was work to be done in my heart in more ways than one! Yes, I see that the necessary tear-down occurred, but now there is a rebuilding going on. I am so grateful to know this, and to look forward to what God is doing. I pray that my heart will be in tune with His as He leads in this process. I trust that you will be praying along with me; and I covenant to hold each of you, my readers, in my own prayers.

If there is a tearing down in your life right now, be assured that what is to follow is a glorious rebuilding. Trust God for that. May He be your constant Guide and Companion in these days.

HOPE

Advent Season is here! So soon it seems, yet there is always a sense of waiting for this time of year, don't you think? I was thinking about this, and it feels as though even shortly after the New Year we are heading into "how many days until Christmas." To my mind it also echoes the heartbeat of our faith: waiting. Hope is a big part of waiting, I've decided to concentrate on hope. On my bathroom wall, the following words are framed. I see them every day, but don't always *notice* them, if you know what I mean. They are from Psalm 33:20-22. "Our soul waits for the LORD, He is our help and our shield. For our heart shall rejoice in Him, because we have trusted in His holy name. Let Your mercy, O LORD, be upon us, just as we hope in You." Waiting and trusting bring hope to my soul, as difficult as they sometimes can be.

Now, as Christmas approaches, hope rises with the promise of Jesus, who was born like us, to die for us. His birth set events into motion that will someday bring us the fulfillment of that promise, and the realization of the hope we hold on to with all our hearts. A timely signpost this week--**HOPE**.

I found a quote from Barbara Johnson, beloved member of the Women of Faith team. "Without hope, days are dark. Without hope, we're heartsick. But with hope we can know Christ's joy no matter what obstacles we face. As someone said, 'In Christ we have a love that cannot be fathomed, a joy that cannot be diminished, and a hope that can never be disappointed.' Instead of a hopeless end, we have endless hope!"[xvii]

Here are my thoughts on having hope at Christmas:

HOPE
Into the chill of December
comes the warmth of chiming bells;

a Christmas carillon.
Senses enhanced by anticipation
embrace the sound
as bells ring from street corner
to church steeple
summoning hope…
in the eyes of a child
filled with expectant desire;
in the heart of the downtrodden
longing for transformation;
in the soul of a hurting world
hungering for peace;
The music peals for all.
The eyes of our Heavenly Father look down in love.
The heart of a Savior beats with longing.
The Prince of Peace says, "Come."
And hope rings the bells!

"…looking for that blessed hope and glorious appearing of our great God and Savior Jesus Christ, who gave Himself for us, that He might redeem us from every lawless deed and purify for Himself *His* own special people, zealous for good works." Titus 2:13

May you grab hold of hope and hang on tightly! I'm certainly trying to do just that.

OKAY!

I greet you on this last day of the year with mingled amazement and praise. Amazed at how quickly this strange year has passed, and praise for all the ways that God has touched my life. And hopefully, because of His work in mine, your lives have been touched as well.

I found my signpost for this week as I was chatting with a friend last week. She was describing the children's Christmas program at her church. They had placed the "angel" on a chair to raise her above Mary and Joseph, and from that perch, she gravely announced to Mary, "You're going to have a baby." To which Mary replied, "Okay." Then the angel turned to Joseph, "And you're going to be the baby's daddy," and Joseph answered, "Okay." We stood there and chuckled, visualizing the scene, but at the same time, comprehending the simplicity and beauty of their childlike responses. My signpost, as strange as it may sound, is **OKAY.**

Pondering that little story on Christmas morning, I turned in my Bible to Luke 1, and read again the story of Mary's hearing of the announcement from the angel Gabriel. Her response awakened a song of joy in my own heart. Mary said in Luke 1:38, "Behold the maidservant of the Lord! Let it be to me according to Your word." In essence, "Okay." I read on. "My soul magnifies the Lord, and my spirit has rejoiced in God my Savior. For He has regarded the lowly state of His maidservant; for behold, henceforth all generations will call me blessed. For He who is mighty has done great things for me, and holy is His name." Luke 1:46-49.

I want Mary's song to be my song as well. She had the ultimate blessing to carry God's Son to His birth, which is why we call her blessed. I realized that I, too, am blessed to have so many opportunities to carry His word, His hope, His joy and peace wherever I go; to whomever I meet. I wrote in my journal, "You, my mighty God, have done great things for me and gratefully I praise You, holy is Your name. I will trust in You."

I wish you each and every one a blessed, joyful, peace-filled New Year. At the cusp of a brand new year, may we who know Him realize that we have opportunity after opportunity to carry the word of God to those still awaiting the miracle of new birth. Personally, my prayer is this for a new year: "Behold the maidservant of the Lord! Let it be to me according to Your word." Whatever, wherever, whoever, Father, **OKAY**!

ANCHOR

Greetings! Well, the first week of the New Year is tucked away under our belts. How is it going for you? I have found myself leaping in anticipation *and* plunging into discouragement, depending on circumstances—my circumstances partly being what the scale says in the morning. Is it a gain or loss? Or the discouragement comes with pain that has kept me from doing what I need to do, like exercise. I have something wrong with my feet that has really hampered the efforts to do what is necessary to keep improving my health and stamina. And I've again spent a lot of time in the recliner resting, which is probably what is most needful right now, even though I am chafing at the inactivity.

I've talked in the past about choosing my "one perfect word" for the year and am announcing this year's choice. It is HOPE. I've been studying and pondering this word for several weeks now, and it seems appropriate that it will be my focus in the coming year. My verse for the year is Romans 5:5. "Now hope does not disappoint, because the love of God has been poured out in our hearts by the Holy Spirit who was given to us."

You will probably be reading a lot here about hope in the future, because it is where my concentration will be. The Greek definition of hope is: "to anticipate with pleasure; to expect or have confidence in." We find hope and confidence in looking back at God's faithfulness in the past. How fitting for me it is today to look back over the past year. I reflect on the victories, the blessings and trials, looking for the hope that only God provides; the hope that does not disappoint because of the love of God poured out in my heart. And oh, what joy that love has brought me. I will never forget this year.

So you are probably thinking that hope is my signpost for this week. No. Not completely. That's my focus for the year.

There are *another* couple of verses that have grabbed my attention lately. Hebrews 6:17-19a. "Thus God, determining to show more abundantly to the heirs of promise the immutability of His counsel, confirmed it by an oath, that by two immutable things, in which it is impossible for God to lie, we might have strong consolation who have fled for refuge to lay hold of the hope set before us. This hope we have as an anchor of the soul, both sure and steadfast..." My signpost? **ANCHOR**. A sure and steadfast anchor, the hope we have in God's promises. As flippy and floppy, as up and down as I've been this week, the idea of an anchor is so very appealing and I need it. There's an old hymn that has been running through my mind lately, and its final words are: "My anchor holds and grips the solid Rock. This Rock is Jesus, yes, He's the only one. Be very sure, be very sure, your anchor holds and grips the solid Rock."[xviii] I'm holding on. I hope you are as well. Because if you know Him, you have that anchor, too.

BLANKET

I have been on the road for six days and just returned late yesterday. All I could do was sit in my recliner and sleep! There was nothing left in my tank.

I had the opportunity to attend a retreat-planning getaway over the weekend, beginning the process of putting together the September retreat for our church conference women. It is always a joy to be with the ladies on the team with whom I have become very close. This is the fourth retreat I've been involved in planning with them.

Then I came home Sunday evening with just enough time to unpack and repack for a speaking trip; leaving on Monday morning. Both of these trips were fulfilling, spiritually and emotionally, and totally enjoyable, but I have to admit I am just a little slower than I used to be!

Perhaps my signpost for the week might seem a bit whimsical--it is **BLANKET**. What does that conjure up in your mind? We were staying with friends, and my husband was attending an early morning Bible study breakfast with our host. I told him to wake me up so I could have a good quiet time before the speaking event. After he was gone, I snuggled under the weight of warm flannel sheets and soft blankets, and I was so comforted—my thought was that **BLANKET** would be a good signpost for this week.

Wondering why that would pop into my mind; I turned to God's Word (after I reluctantly departed the warm bed) and my thought was of His covering as a blanket, so I went to Psalm 91:4. "He shall cover you with His feathers, and under His wings you shall take refuge; His truth shall be your shield and buckler."

I've memorized this psalm and often recite it when I am trying to fall asleep, so it is very familiar; however there is, as usual upon pondering, a new sweetness to the thought of the soft covering of His feathers. A down comforter and feather pillow was what I had been sleeping with at the other home we were visiting and the bed I had just departed was total comfort. My mind picked up a thread of thought. Here I am far from home, from my own bed; miserable with a painful foot (another story) and yet as I lie in unfamiliar beds, I am covered, comforted and warm. And it brings to my mind the truth of God's Word; that He is with me, His Presence as real as the blankets I've slept under.

Hear again the first two verses of Psalm 91. "He who dwells in the secret place of the Most High shall abide under the shadow of the Almighty. I will say of the LORD, 'He is my refuge and my fortress; my God, in Him will I trust.'" Oh, as I sat there in the breaking daylight my heart was full of God, the reality of Him and the peace of resting under His feathery wings.

Have you found yourself in the secret place of the Most High? It is a wonderful place in which to dwell. I pray that you will secure His promised blanket around you this week, trusting Him and knowing the peace of His covering *you* with His feathers.

TENDER MERCIES

Good Morning. I hope your week is going well. I seem to be struggling right now, not knowing exactly what God would have me say to you. The past couple of weeks have been concentrated on the pain in my foot/ankle, without an answer yet for the cause. Many prayers have gone up, for which I am certainly appreciative but, as so many of you already know, constant pain is debilitating and colors everything else in your life. I'm still waiting to hear from the doctor this morning, so I can't offer any ideas, other than inflammation from the cyst that was lanced, or possibly gout. Whatever, it HURTS! Every step.

So, there it is. Frustration and discouragement, because I have things to do. I chuckled when I happened to glance at Hebrews 12:12 one day last week. I'd been looking at another passage, but then this verse popped up. "Therefore strengthen the hands which hang down, and the feeble knees, and make straight paths for your feet, so that what is lame may not be dislocated, but rather be healed." What a sense of humor God has.

Of course, the writer of Hebrews is speaking of spiritual vitality, but sitting in the chair with throbbing feet, it seemed appropriate. So I will share from my journal ponderings as I was searching to find words from God the other day that touched my heart with regard to my hurting body.

What I found was comfort in Psalm 25:1-2. "To You, O LORD, I lift up my soul. O my God, I trust in You; let me not be ashamed; let not my enemies triumph over me." And further, "Show me your ways, O LORD; teach me Your paths, lead me in Your truth and teach me, for You are the God of my salvation, on You I wait all the day." Psalm 25:4-5. Next to this verse in the margin I had written, "Do I?"

But I read on, and it was Psalm 25:6 that made my eyes

sting with tears. "Remember, O LORD, Your tender mercies and Your lovingkindnesses, for they are from of old." Why did it touch me? I think it's because of the reminder of *where* I am to focus--on His tender mercies, because He has always been there for me. The last half of Psalm 25:7 says, "According to Your mercy, remember me, for Your goodness' sake, O LORD." Again, in the margin I had written "His sake, not mine." I guess the words "tender mercies" resonate with me this morning because I am feeling such pain and discouragement and need a loving touch. What could be more loving than the surety that in His mercy, His tender mercy, He cares for me and He will continue to do so?

I've noticed that with hurting feet, I am constantly looking for shortcuts—how few steps I can take to accomplish something. I don't want to cause myself pain, so I do everything I can not to suffer any more than I have to. Can it be true for us in our spiritual lives as well? There is pain in sacrifice, and the effort to do what is right, but we don't want to do the painful things, we want simply to waltz around them instead, taking shortcuts as it were, to try and reach the healing and peace for which we all long.

Today I asked myself, "What have I learned through this? What is my signpost for the week?" I want to use **TENDER MERCIES**. How precious is God's tenderness with me. The knowledge of His presence, and the comprehension that He is working in my life. So I choose to focus on His tender mercy, rather than on pain (which was my first thought for a signpost)

May God bless you this week in your own pain and healing, wherever you are. May you know the truth of His presence and His **TENDER MERCIES** in your walk with Him.

SATISFACTION

The first order of business this morning is to report that the pain in my foot and ankle is almost entirely gone. I have gout in my ankle which is the culprit, and there are meds for that. So I'm now tapering off a week's dose of Prednisone and able to walk without pain. I cannot tell you how grateful I am for your prayers, as well as a diagnosis and medication.

I was blessed to hold a workshop last week for a women's ministry group and I so appreciate your prayers for me. They have invited me back and I am thrilled. It seems that God is opening so many doors right now. My sister wrote and told me I'd better slow down because my body didn't seem to be handling things very well, but I told her I am holding on to God's hand and don't want to miss a single blessing He has for me!

As each week begins I look for a word from God, something to share with you, something that I can use for a signpost on this healing journey. I think I have found it this morning. It is **SATISFACTION**. Searching through the Psalms, as I often do to begin my quiet time, I found one of my favorites, which begins, "O God, You are my God; early will I seek you; my soul thirsts for You; my flesh longs for You in a dry and thirsty land where there is no water. So I have looked for You in the sanctuary, to see Your power and Your glory. Because Your lovingkindness is better than life, my lips shall praise You. Thus I will bless You while I live; I will lift up my hands in Your name. My soul shall be satisfied as with marrow and fatness and my mouth shall praise You with joyful lips." Psalm 63:1-5.

A rather long passage, but I want to share with you the progression I discovered in these verses. First, longing and thirst; which is so necessary because without it we wouldn't seek Him. When we seek Him we find that He (His lovingkindness, mercy, etc.) is better than life.

When finding this to be true, our lips respond in praise, the proper glorifying response to a revelation of Himself. And our souls are satisfied. From thirst to satisfaction. From longing to fulfilment. A journey. An interrupted journey, just as our physical life's journeys often are, but a journey to be undertaken for the joy that awaits us. A long time ago I prayed, "God, please make me desire you." It was then that my own personal journey toward intimacy began; as it must for all of us. Thirst for Him, and longing is placed inside each one of us when God breathes our life into being. My prayer is that you will recognize and acknowledge that thirst and come to know Him more and more, that your soul will be satisfied in much the same way as a good meal satisfies your body. Then, and only then, comes true praise from joyful lips!

May God's rich blessings rest upon each one of you!

WAITING

Greetings from a place of disappointment. Sorry to report that the foot pain is back with a vengeance and I am headed to the doctor today. It is wearing me out, and the worst part is that I can't exercise and I definitely feel that lack. I'm afraid I'm going to have to start all over! Please pray that we will find a solution.

With that in mind, I'm declaring my signpost for the week. It is **WAITING**. Such a difficult discipline to cultivate. For the past few days I have been pondering on the subject of healing, going through my Bible looking for verses that mention it, mainly I guess, because I've been hurting.

Isaiah 30 speaks much about it, healing I mean; and I was intrigued to read verse 18 and the last part of verse 19, "Therefore the LORD will wait, that He may be gracious to you; and therefore He will be exalted, that He may have mercy on you. For the LORD is a God of justice; blessed are all those who wait for Him. He will be very gracious to you at the sound of your cry; when He hears it, He will answer you." I find this so very comforting. That God will wait, so that He can be gracious to me. I gather that there are instances when I am in a place where He can't bless me for whatever reason, probably due to my not being in good communication with Him.

What rings through here is His desire to bless, to be gracious to His people. He **waits** to hear our cry. When we absorb this truth, our cries indicate that our hearts are **waiting** on Him, depending on Him for His mercy and grace, rather than our own efforts. So I am thinking that it's important that I be sure to be **waiting** on Him.

I went back and re-read Chapter 30:15. "For thus says the Lord GOD, the Holy One of Israel: 'In returning and rest you shall be saved; in quietness and confidence shall be your strength.' But you would not." And I wonder, am I chafing under the imposed inactivity? Am I impatient to get moving again; and not submitting to the need for rest for my foot to recover? It could be that it would heal if I would stay off of it and quit stressing it.

Anyway, it seems to me that God is saying, "**Wait** on Me. Rest, find your strength in being close to Me." Maybe the doctor will have some instructions for me--my physical self, I mean!

This application is true in the spiritual sense I believe, as well as in the physical. Rushing about putting stress and strain on parts that may be weaker brings on pain, and only in calmness and rest do we find the strength to carry on.

As I read this over, it sounds a lot like whining! And I know that many of you are struggling with far, far worse situations, so I feel a little silly complaining. However, my goal in sharing my thoughts with you is to encourage you to hear God's voice speaking through your own issues, and to seek Him. He **waits** for you to do so. I leave you with this from further down in the 30th chapter of Isaiah, verse 26. "Moreover the light of the moon will be as the light of the sun, and the light of the sun will be sevenfold, as the light of seven days, in the day that the LORD binds up the bruise of His people and heals the stroke of their wound." This is what we ultimately have to look forward to. And oh, what a day that will be!

SHOWERS OF BLESSING

Hello! I've been thinking all morning about just what to say today. It's always exciting (I get a thrill out of a blank piece of paper) to start considering the message I feel God is laying on my heart.

I collect sheep. For many years I have been gifted with hundreds of sheep items: figurines, pictures, quotes, and this collection is very precious to me. A lot of these things have come from all over the world, as my sister and her husband consistently pick up some sort of sheep memorabilia for me whenever they travel. Not only do I enjoy having these sheep, I am constantly reminded as I look at them how God uses the images of sheep and shepherd to describe His interaction in our lives. We have much to learn from sheep because we are so much like them. But that's a whole other story...

As I was reading in the book of Ezekiel the other day, I discovered the following passage from Chapter 34:11-12. "Thus says the Lord GOD, 'Indeed I Myself will search for My sheep and seek them out. As a shepherd seeks out his flock on the day he is among his scattered sheep, so will I seek out My sheep and deliver them from all the places where they were scattered on a cloudy and dark day.'" The prophet continues "I will make a covenant of peace with them...and I will cause showers to come down in their season, there shall be showers of blessing.'" Ezekiel 34:25a and 26b.

Do you ever feel as though you have been "scattered on a cloudy and dark day?" I know I have, and so the promises God makes here are sweet to my soul. Perhaps those of us who live in Washington can comprehend this better than those in sunny climates. He promises to search for us, seek us, and deliver us from those dark places. He then promises a covenant of peace with us; which He has fulfilled in sending Jesus as our savior.

I am reminded of Ephesians 2:14. "For He Himself (Jesus) is our peace who has made both one, and has broken down the middle wall of separation." And Ephesians 2:17 "And He came and preached peace to you who were afar off and those who were near. For through Him we both have access by one Spirit to the Father."

And then, **then**! Hear again the words of this old hymn: "There shall be showers of blessing; this is the promise of love; there shall be seasons refreshing, sent from the Savior above."[xix] This is my weekly signpost. **SHOWERS OF BLESSING**. I see in my mind's eye a verdant meadow, freshly washed by a cleansing rain, where we as God's children, His sheep, will be able to rest; reveling in being searched out, delivered, and restored. Sort of a Psalm 23 place, I guess! How wonderful, when life tosses us a curve or things seem dismal to call this picture to mind, and look to our Father as He seeks us. I am so grateful for the Scriptures that paint in words a canvas that stretches across the sky, declaring the greatest love of all.

Is your life seemingly stuck in a cloudy and dark place? There is a nail-pierced hand reaching out, searching for you. Grab hold. He will never let go.

UNDERSTANDING

Good day to you! I'm still fighting the gout flare and getting discouraged, I'll admit. Nothing seems to be working and every step hurts terribly. God however is meeting me here in this place, and as the psalmist says in Psalm 42:5, "Why are you cast down O my soul? And why are you disquieted within me. Hope in God, for I will yet praise Him for the help of His countenance." Ironically I was reading in Job and found this beautiful promise in Chapter 8:21. "He will yet fill your mouth with singing and your lips with rejoicing." One doesn't expect a nugget of joy in a book filled with woe and suffering but nevertheless, there it is. And I'm clinging to it.

The other day in *Jesus Calling* I found these words: "Thank Me for the conditions that are requiring you to be still. Do not spoil these quiet hours by wishing them away, waiting impatiently to be active again."^{xx} Ouch! "I'm so chafing under this crippled foot business," I prayed, "and I should thank You?"

I read on. Someone was speaking straight to my heart. "Instead of resenting the limitations of a weakened body, search for My way in the midst of these very circumstances."^{xxi} I was reminded of another favorite verse, Isaiah 30:15. "In returning and rest you shall be saved; in quietness and confidence shall be your strength." It says that strength will be found <u>in</u> quietness and confidence. Is it saying to me that this time of enforced rest can strengthen and build my trust in God? Perhaps my moaning and groaning are fruitless; I must turn them into gratitude, that His purpose in me be fulfilled. Can I really say "Thank you for this gout?"

I was struck this morning by the truth that I CAN walk. It hurts, but I can do it. And gratitude filled me. My prayer, then, instead of whining for relief, is to ask for God's help to search His way in the midst of it, and to look forward to what He desires to teach me.

My signpost for this week is **UNDERSTANDING**, as in this verse from Psalm 119:73, "Your hands have made me and fashioned me; give me understanding that I may learn Your commandments." Oh, yes! A prayer that God will delight to answer. Is it yours, too? I pray that it is.

MISERY

Shakespeare wrote in Macbeth of "Sleep that knits up the raveled sleeve of care."[xxii] If that is true, I must have a whole sweater! It seems that ever since I got home Saturday night from a speaking event, I have been doing nothing but sleeping. Shakespeare's meaning for these words is that sleep has a way of gentling our cares and smoothing out things that are confusing. For me, though, I am simply exhausted.

Perhaps I overextended myself on the weekend, but it was worth it! The event was all I hoped it would be and I am so grateful to God for the blessings of that day. Thank you for your prayers; they are so appreciated. The pain and swelling in my foot by the time I got home were intense, but prayer and a gracious God got me through.

Sunday morning I woke up with the disease of the week-- a stuffy nose and sore throat. So probably it isn't strange that my signpost for the week is **MISERY.** Everybody knows what it's like to be sick, to have the flu, right? I slept most of the day and am still feeling pretty rotten, falling asleep every time I sit down. So, I will be brief today. No energy or inspiration it seems, only my asking once *again* for your prayers for the weekend. I am speaking this week on Saturday at a Women's Tea. Obviously, the needs are for healing of the cold and for the energy to prepare, as well as pain relief enough that I can actually do it. God is good, and over and over again He has met whatever need I have for a particular event, but it never hurts to keep praying in faith. So thank you all who send those requests toward heaven.

On the foot/ankle front, my doctor is referring me to an orthopedic doc, as he feels that if it were just gout, it would be better by now, so something else may be going on.

I want to share with you the verses that are holding me up

80

this week in the midst of a great deal of frustration and misery.

Although I have shared them with you before, they are important in my life. Hear them once more from Psalm 33:20-22. "Our soul waits for the LORD; He is our help and our shield. For our heart shall rejoice in Him, because we have trusted in His holy name. Let Your mercy, O LORD, be upon us, just as we hope in You." May my **MISERY** be tempered with His mercy.

Looking forward to what the next few days will bring, and sending you all blessings and hugs.

REASSURANCE

First, I have to thank you to all who prayed about last Saturday. God did show up, and I made it through the event without coughing and with energy, if not healing. I'm still fighting the after-effects of the cold, but feeling a bit better every day. Unfortunately my husband has caught the bug from me and is totally miserable. We are sticking very close to the house lately.

I did, however, visit the orthopedic clinic. The first doctor I saw looked at the X-rays they took and said that there is nothing wrong in my ankle--no broken bones or anything like that. He was not sure just what is causing all the pain and swelling, only that it is no doubt gout-related, and he is not an expert on that. So he wants me to be seen by another doctor, who is, as he puts it, the "best foot and ankle guy" he knows. The new doctor needed an MRI, and believe it or not, they got me in for an MRI that same day! A small miracle. God be praised.

Now I am waiting until next Tuesday for the results and appointment with the new doctor. Though I can't share any good news with you yet, let's pray that next week there will be something.

For some reason, I have a fear of going to the doctor! This time was no exception, and I didn't rest well the night before. Questioning this as I wrote in my journal on Monday morning — I asked, "Why am I so afraid?" It never is as bad as I envision it to be. I realized I was caught between the concern that they wouldn't find anything that they could cure, and that they would find something serious.

In my mind, a cortisone shot would qualify as something tough to endure, and I wanted Fred to be there to hold my hand. He was sick, though, and not feeling up to sitting in the waiting room and coughing. So as I journaled I prayed, "Father, You are going to have to hold my hand and give me courage and strength."

I was paging through my Bible and my eye caught these words from Psalm 73:23, "Nevertheless, I am continually with You; You hold me by my right hand." Words just for me! I had been looking for Psalm 56:3 to note in my journal, "Whenever I am afraid, I will trust in You." Both of these verses ministered to me, because I *was* afraid, but God knew I needed His reassurance. Of course, the doctor visit was not bad at all.

I think my signpost for the week is **REASSURANCE**. How sweet to be assured of His answer to my need, even though it might seem a small, silly concern. I love that about God: His personal presence every moment, and how He shows that reality over and over again. Have you felt that reassurance? I hope so, because it is a marvelous faith-builder.

Once again may I ask for your prayers as I speak at a mini-retreat Friday and Saturday. Thank you. I pray that God will bless your life with richness because of your faithfulness to carry me to the Throne of Grace. Each prayer is surely appreciated.

HEALTHY

Greetings! I hope you are all having a great day. I find myself once more wanting to express my appreciation to all who prayed for me over the weekend. God was amazing in that He kept me from coughing during all four of my presentations and the ladies were so gracious to let me wear my bedroom slippers because I couldn't get my shoe on. My ankle was *very* swollen. So I do appreciate your faithful prayers.

The visit to the doctor didn't offer very much in the way of answers. I am having more blood tests and they took a bunch more X-rays. Diagnosis: basically gouty arthritis. But no consensus of how to treat it, so I was disappointed a bit. I am encouraged this morning because it doesn't hurt nearly as bad as it has been. Perhaps the combination of staying off it and the medicine I've already been taking is working at last. I can only hope.

My last few posts seem to have all been about the physical struggles and a lot of whining and complaining. I have been very discouraged--my life seeming to be on hold, just trying to get **HEALTHY**. I'm using that word as my signpost this week. It seems such a hard goal to reach. It is one of my year goals, however, to fully recover from the heart surgery, becoming firmly entrenched in an exercise discipline. Which is why the discouragement steals in. For almost three months I have hardly been able to walk around the house, let alone around the block! And I feel far from even *beginning* to reach my goal. But there must be something I need to learn and I am submitting to the process of truly trusting God. I'm feeling more hopeful than last week--anchored in this promise from Psalm 31:24. "Be of good courage and He shall strengthen your heart, all you who hope in the LORD."

REVIVE

Today I find myself writing from a heavy spirit. I'm not sure why, because my foot is decidedly better, and the coughing and cold misery is diminishing.

I always desire my blog posts to be uplifting and encouraging, to myself as well as to my readers, but to be perfectly honest, this week I am experiencing a profound sense of discouragement and weakness to the point of actually feeling depressed. I hate to admit it, but I can't get around it, so I am asking once more for your prayers as I try to regain my strength and purpose. When you feel like this (and I'm sure you all have at some point), it seems lame to say it, because so many others have issues and cares much more intense than mine. However, the truth is that we all have valleys to slog through, and perhaps this is the promised grief and depression as a result of the heart surgery. They said it could happen, even up to a year. So, there it is. And I am depending on your prayer support, because I am trusting God to bring me through. If it doesn't go away soon, I promise I will ask for help. But for today, this is the way it is.

I have been spending time in Psalm 119, and the word that is sticking out to me is found several times. **REVIVE.** And my prayer is that God will, in His faithfulness, revive not only my physical weakness, but my spirit as well. Let me share a few verses that have ministered to me lately: Psalm 119:73, 75-77 "Your hands have made me and fashioned me; give me understanding, that I may learn Your commandments. I know, O LORD, that Your judgments are right, and that in faithfulness You have afflicted me. Let, I pray, Your merciful kindness be for my comfort, according to Your word to Your servant. Let Your tender mercies come to me, that I may live; for Your law is my delight."

I'm happy for the improvement in the physical issues,

believe me. And hopefully it will continue.

"Revive me, O LORD, for Your name's sake! For Your righteousness' sake, bring my soul out of trouble." Psalm 143:11. This is my prayer as well as my signpost. **REVIVE** me, please.

NO DISAPPOINTMENT

This is a much better week, thank God! Things are definitely looking up. The cough lingers, but I'm feeling a whole lot healthier, and the swelling from the gout continues to subside and I am walking with only the barest limp. A lot of Hallelujahs! And as health improves, my spirits lift. I'm still battling the low mood, but it is really improving.

Perhaps some of that is due to finally getting out of the house! I was able to attend church for the first time in five weeks, and we were able to get our income taxes prepared and my driver's license renewed, groceries in the house, and one chorus rehearsal attended! Couldn't really sing much without coughing, but it was great to see everybody and hear the music we are supposed to be learning. So there is a feeling of accomplishment instead of a sense of despair at my physical weakness.

My word, my one perfect word for this year is "Hope," and I want to keep it always in the forefront of my mind. I saw a quote by Emily Dickinson that I think is beautiful: "Hope is a thing with feathers that perches in the soul, and sings the tune without the words, and never stops at all."[xxiii] I like the imagery of a little bird of hope in my soul who never stops singing. It brings to my mind my verse for the year from Romans 5:5. "Now hope does not disappoint because the love of God has been poured out in our hearts by the Holy Spirit who was given to us."

The kind of hope that lasts, and never disappoints, is based on the promises of God in His word, and when we lose sight of that, our spirits tend to droop because of circumstances. A few days after I wrote last week's post, I was reading *Jesus Calling* and found an answer to my doldrums. "I shower blessings on you daily, but sometimes you don't perceive them. When your mind is stuck on a negative focus, you see neither Me nor My gifts."[xxiv]

My signpost for the week is **NO DISAPPOINTMENT**. It is a reminder to me that I have laid aside the promise of my verse for the year. Disappointment is lurking in my subconscious and I have had to confess that I have been inviting it inside.

But with a concentrated renewed focus on Jesus, my hope is restored. If any of you are struggling with hopelessness, may I encourage you to, (as the old hymn says) "turn your eyes upon Jesus; look full in His wonderful face. And the things of earth will grow strangely dim, in the light of His glory and grace."[xxv] With a lighter heart, I thank God for His grace, and I thank you, too for your upholding prayers.

PLEASURES

Greetings. I've been gone from home the past couple of days, helping a friend who had knee replacement surgery, keeping her company, helping with her meals and meds, etc.

It's been a great week! On top of feeling so much better, I celebrated my birthday on Monday and was so blessed by many greetings and cards and phone calls. We were treated to a great dinner on Sunday evening with dear friends, and Fred took me back to Red Lobster for dinner on my actual birthday. My favorite restaurant. And coconut shrimp, my very favorite food. Who wouldn't feel special and blessed, I ask you!

God has blessed me this week, as well, with the messages I have found in His word. I opened my copy of *Jesus Calling* on Monday, and found some of my most precious verses. For instance, Jeremiah 29:13-14a: "'And you will seek Me and find Me, when you search for Me with all your heart. I will be found by you', says the LORD..." and this one, Deuteronomy 33:27, "The eternal God is your refuge, and underneath are the everlasting arms." Such comforting and uplifting words on my special day. And then I opened my Bible (currently I am going through the Bible looking at "joy" passages), and what should pop up Monday morning but Psalm 16:11. "You will show me the path of life; in your presence is fullness of joy; at your right hand are pleasures forevermore."

This reference is inscribed in every copy of my first book, *Psalms From the Pathway*. It is one that is special to me, notwithstanding the beauty of the words themselves. Being reminded of it on my birthday was a sweet gift from my Heavenly Father, and I am very grateful. What follows is a comment made on this verse that I offer as encouragement to myself as well as to each one of you.

Quoting Dee Brestin: "Run after God the way you did when you first fell in love. Wake up talking to Him, thanking Him, asking for direction for your day and expect to hear from Him; watch for Him, talk with Him in the night. Set the Lord always before you and He will fill you with joy and with pleasures forever more."[xxvi]

It seems that doing all this would bring a life of joy, and that is my goal! **PLEASURES.** The signpost for my week.

RELIEF

I certainly hope this week finds you in peak condition. It's so good to report that things around here are definitely improving. I actually went to the water aerobics class yesterday, as well as a chorus rehearsal. It was so good to be back in the pool *and* the hot tub. I have really missed this when I wasn't feeling well enough to exercise. Now I can restart a rehab routine and get back to working on my recovery, which is one of my goals this year.

So it is with relief and joy that I write this morning. Relief and gratitude for healing. Joy for remembering Easter and what we celebrate. Joy for the forgiveness and love that characterizes my relationship with my Heavenly Father--joy that beats in my heart with the realization of God's promises of His presence. I was reading the 32nd Psalm the other day--a beautiful passage, a contemplation of David.

And as I contemplated also, I found much cause for rejoicing! The psalm begins with this, "Blessed is he whose transgression is forgiven, whose sin is covered." Psalm 32:1. It then talks about the joy of confession in verse 5 and how God surrounds us with songs of deliverance. He is our hiding place in verse 7. I find this so precious.

He also promises to instruct us in the way we should go, to guide us with His eye, in verse 8. The psalm ends with these words in verse 11, "Be glad in the LORD and rejoice, you righteous; and shout for joy, all you upright in heart!" You'll have to read the whole psalm for yourself to get the impact. As I read through these verses over and over, I reflected upon how I could not help but rejoice and be glad when I absorbed the rest of the truths expressed in the content of the psalm.

I am so grateful for the word of God and how it touches

upon every aspect of life, bringing comfort and encouragement when our souls are weary. I think **RELIEF** is a good word to reflect upon for my signpost this week. I truly hope you find relief to be real in your life. Relief for any burden you may be carrying. Just open yourself to the beauty of a God who cares intimately for each and every one of us.

CARRIED

Good Morning! I have had a wonderful week. I hope the same is true for you. As I go through the days and ponder on God's faithfulness and the blessings He gives, I usually wonder, "What shall I write about today?"

No problem this week. I was so excited to hear Carol Kent speak again. A local church invited her to come for the weekend and share about healing relationships. I was privileged to get to know her as our speaker for the women's retreat last September. Let me put in a commercial here--if you ever get a chance to read any of her books or hear her speak, I encourage you to do so. She is an amazing woman of God with an incredible story to tell.

Friday, Saturday and Sunday I spent hearing God speak to my heart through her words, and feel so blessed to have had this opportunity, as well as the joy of reconnecting with friends I rarely see. Additionally this week marks the 1-year anniversary of my heart issues. One year ago yesterday I entered the hospital, and next Tuesday will be the surgery anniversary. It is a time to contemplate just what this year has been, pondering about the changes in me, the healing process, and simply the joy of being alive.

Many of you have shared this journey with me and I am so grateful for each one of you. This morning I was reading Holley Gerth's blog, *Coffee For Your Heart*, a truly encouraging post, wherein she spoke of the importance of feeling free to call for backup. I was especially struck by her words, "We're made to share life with each other. We're made to say, 'I need you. Please help me.'[xxvii] Contrary to our opinion sometimes, Holley continues: "Those aren't words of weakness—they're the strongest words we can say. It's easy to try to figure things out on our own. It's much harder to say, 'Please carry my heart to Jesus today.'"xxviii

As I read her thoughts, I was so aware of how many of you have *carried my heart to Jesus*, and I am so exceedingly grateful. I have saved all of the cards sent to me throughout the surgery and ensuing recovery. Over this next week, I plan to go over each one, savoring the heartfelt words of comfort and prayer and rejoicing with each memory.

It IS going to be a celebration next Tuesday (Fred promised) and I invite you to lift up your own hearts in praise, because you all are a part of it. May God bless you for what you have done for me. "We give thanks to You, O God, we give thanks! For Your wondrous works declare that Your name is near." Psalm 75:1

Musing over this year, my signpost for today is **CARRIED**. I think it's a good way to express my heart's gratitude for your faithfulness to pray for me! Because I have very definitely felt that uplifting sensation of being carried on wings of prayer. My heart is full.

SURGI-VERSARY

Greetings. I told you last week that we would celebrate the **SURGI-VERSARY** this week, one year today! We made it to water aerobics this morning, which is a celebration in itself and was so enjoyable. We didn't notice the time until it was almost too late to go, so had to forego breakfast. Suffice it to say that we were pretty hungry when we got home.

Fred said, "How would you like to go to your favorite restaurant for lunch?" It only took a second or two to say "Yes!" Any time we go there it's a celebration. I love the food, and love the hugs from all the people I used to work with prior to my surgery. After lunch most of the rest of the day was spent working on a talk I'm giving Saturday at a Dessert Social. By the way, I would ask for your prayers for me for that event.

I capped off the day by spending the evening re-reading all the cards received during and after my hospital stay. I never threw a single one away, and it was pure joy to visit those days in memory, to hear again the thoughts and prayers that had been extended. I am extremely grateful for so many loving remarks and encouraging words. God is indeed good, and I appreciate each and every card and message.

This completes my first year of the journey God has prescribed for me--a new heart and hopefully a new message of His gracious care. I have looked for signposts along the way and written my observations on the highway, harking back to the verse that really began my weekly blogging of the road signs. "Set up *signposts*, make landmarks; set your heart toward the highway, the way in which you went." Jeremiah 31:21

I will, of course, continue to write. I thank all you faithful ones who keep reading it and I promise to be with you in word and in spirit in the weeks ahead. I know there will be signposts to observe.

Truly I am feeling anticipation for what lies in the future, and though the one-year journey of recovery is behind me, I am rejoicing in the fact that I am alive, filled with hope and joy! I celebrate you and the ways in which you have blessed me.

"I thank my God upon every remembrance of you, always in every prayer of mine making request for you all with joy, for your fellowship in the gospel from the first day until now, being confident of this very thing, that He who has begun a good work in you will complete it until the day of Jesus Christ; just as it is right for me to think this of you all, because I have you in my heart..." Philippians 1:3-7a.

This speaks my heart to you, my friends.

FAITHFUL

It was beautifully sunny when I got up, but now the clouds have gathered and some of the brightness is covered. I can't help but think that sometimes that's what happens in our lives. We wake to glowing sunshine, anticipation running high…and then a cloud comes over. Perhaps we get bad news, or something frustrating happens, and dimness occurs in our soul. We just have to remember that always the sun waits behind any cloud because Jesus, the Son, will never leave us or forsake us. That hope is what sustains us, and can lift our spirits. I must hold on to that whenever I am tempted to let the disappointment or discouragement take over. I hope you do, too.

Not that I am in any way feeling those "D" words this week. It has been a great few days in many ways. God has been good--the Women's Tea event was an absolute joy. Six women indicated that they had invited Jesus into their hearts as a result, which is very affirming and exciting.

It was additionally enjoyable spending the day with my daughter-in-law, Patricia, who graciously came from Seattle to drive me to the location of the tea.

I have another event this week, an out-of-town all-day retreat. So once again I am asking for prayer. I plan to be speaking on God's abundance and as I have been preparing, it has become very real to ponder on the abundance of His mercy, His provision and best of all, His peace. I am so truly grateful for these opportunities to share!

I'm asking for prayer for safety in travel as we are taking the whole weekend as a bit of a getaway. Prayers too are needed for clarity of thought, and for my heart to be receptive to the Spirit's movement. Further, for inspiration, and that I bring the words that God wants the ladies to hear. Thank you for holding me up.

As I was getting ready to head out to my speaking engagement last week, hearing the enemy try to discourage me, one of the members of the planning team at the church shared Isaiah 41:9-10 with me. I've often repeated verse 10 to myself when I get nervous, but had never connected it to verse 9. Here are both verses: "You whom I have taken from the ends of the earth, and called from its farthest regions, and said to you, 'You are My servant, I have chosen you and have not cast you away: Fear not, for I am with you; be not dismayed, for I am your God. I will strengthen you, yes, I will help you, I will uphold you with My righteous right hand.'"

"Let us hold fast the confession of our hope without wavering, for He who promised is faithful." Hebrews 10:23. I gratefully announce the word **FAITHFUL** as my weekly signpost. There is such encouragement and promise in these verses and I offer them today to you that you can cling to them as the events of your life play out and you need some strength to keep going. God is **FAITHFUL**!

YET

Hello. It seems time has a way of inexorably moving on, doesn't it? And sometimes we have to run to catch up. Such seems to have been the way of things around here lately.

But I'm happy to be here thinking how I can communicate to you the incredible love and generosity of our God, as it has been shown me this week. First of all, thank you for your prayers. I certainly felt each one of them. As I was preparing for the women attending the coming retreat, I felt myself in a strange state of mind. I worked hard on the talks and the Power Point presentation, yet there was a sort of detachment. I couldn't seem to comprehend just what I was trying to say.

Over and over I studied the words, yet when I closed the notebook, I forgot everything. I told Fred as we headed north on Friday that I had seldom felt so unprepared. Either I was totally trusting God, or I was falling apart...I wasn't sure which! But as prayers went up and God's hand reached down, there was peace, and as I said to someone, "I just showed up, and God showed off." Honestly I hope that is the case every time I pick up a microphone. It turned out to be one of the most enjoyable events ever and I am so grateful for the prayers that surrounded me.

Now I have some time ahead for R&R, and it's so welcome. There are ideas and words swirling in my head that I want to explore, plus some lingering household tasks. I'm more excited about the first than the last, obviously! But I am relieved to look down the road and see spaces for growth and study, without pressure to prepare or perform.

Yesterday morning I was drawn to Habakkuk, chapter 3. A small book of a somewhat obscure prophet, yet filled with hope, especially at the end. Verses 17 and 18 are precious, titled in my Bible *A Hymn of Faith*, and indeed it is. "Though the fig tree may not blossom, nor fruit be on the vines; though the labor of the olive may fail, and the fields yield no food; though the flock may be cut off from the fold, and there be no herd in the stalls — yet I will rejoice in the LORD, I will joy in the God of my salvation. The LORD God is my strength; He will make my feet like deer's feet, and He will make me walk on my high hills." Habakkuk describes a terrible scenario of famine and loss. If that were to happen to us, how desperate I imagine we would feel. And he says **YET.** I love that! In spite of everything messed up around me, "I will rejoice." It seems like a good signpost for this week.

Sometimes as I look at dryness in my soul, the temptation arises to complain and groan about what I think are lacks in my life. I've been feeling that way the last couple of days, probably a letdown. So, reading this passage challenges me to rejoice-- whatever. God will strengthen and uphold, and restore and revive my soul. I'm not sure what is ahead, but I AM assured that He will enable me to walk on my high hills, whatever they may be. **YET** I will rejoice.

Thanks for the opportunity to connect with you. I pray God's richest blessings on each one of you.

JOY BURSTS

Wow! This week has been a week of celebration for our family. Our first-born son's birthday, our youngest son and wife's anniversary, our daughter-in-law's birthday and Mother's Day as well. A lot of back and forth phone calls, speaking the appropriate greetings and singing the occasional Happy Birthdays. We were not able to be together last weekend, but have been and will be with both families--one family the week before last and the other this week. I am grateful for the opportunities to celebrate milestones and special days--the joys of being a family.

Speaking of joy, I have been thinking about it, and thankfully experiencing it as well. Lately it seems to be splashing into my heart at unexpected times and in unexpected ways. And I was thinking how refreshing it is to feel a burst of joy. I was reading the book of Philemon in the New Testament, a beautiful story. My heart was captured by a couple of verses that linked love and joy and refreshment, which just solidified my thoughts. "For we have great joy and consolation in your love, because the hearts of the saints have been refreshed by you, brother." Philemon 1:7. What a commendation. How wonderful it would be if that could be said of us--that we have refreshed someone and brought joy, simply by our love. The Apostle Paul begins the closing of his short letter to his friend Philemon in verse 20. "Yes, brother, let me have joy from you in the Lord; refresh my heart in the Lord."

Nicole Johnson of Women of Faith writes: "Joy catches us off guard. It is a response that wells up in our heart from love...we don't find joy; it finds us, often surprising us when it arrives—making us smile for no apparent reason. If you know love, you'll be surprised by joy."[xxix]

Mother's Day, birthdays, anniversaries are occasions for *joy bursts* and, praise God, they have been exploding like fireworks in my heart. Refreshing, renewing, reviving **JOY BURSTS!** I am filled with such thanksgiving. How about that for a signpost? Yes, it has been a good week. You refresh me by your presence in my life, as well.

PRESENCE

Greetings. Last week was busier than I expected. There were opportunities to speak that I had not planned on, but God was great in His supply of energy and I certainly enjoyed the spontaneity that He undergirds, and am ever so grateful to God for bringing occasions like this into my life.

There is good news in the gout department. The pain is nearly gone and the swelling greatly reduced, so walking is much easier. I hope to be back in the exercise routine soon. The bad news is that the cough/cold issue has reared its ugly head again. I'm feeling much like I did earlier this year with the constant cough and runny nose--all those miserable symptoms. I'm wondering just when I will ever again feel good all over.

To be honest, I'm really struggling with these health issues, fighting discouragement. There is so much I want to do and my energy level is flagging. There are concert performances coming up and a road trip to Oregon in June where I will be speaking in three different cities. So, believe me, I need your prayers!

Searching the scriptures lately, I have been greatly comforted by the promises of God's presence. Particularly, yesterday morning as I read anew words that have always been precious. I am clinging to them. In Exodus, when Moses pleads with God to go with His people so all would know they *were* His people, God replies, "My Presence will go with you, and I will give you rest." Exodus 33:14. Isn't that a great signpost? **PRESENCE.**

Right now, I need both His Presence *and* rest--I am promised them. So I will take heart, try to rest and get better, and celebrate the truth that He is WITH me. Hallelujah! May you, too, lean on Him in every circumstance of your own life.

FASTENED

I've just returned from the dentist and have a half-numb mouth. My husband and I both had appointments and work done. I am so relieved that I got through it without coughing. I was praying the whole time that the urge to cough be removed until they were done and all the junk and metal removed from my mouth. I didn't start the coughing spasms until it was all over. Thank You, God.

I hesitate to write today, but I promised. I'm trying to be positive and upbeat and offer something to encourage myself, as well as you readers. I have not felt positive in any way this week, in fact, just the opposite. I'm struggling again with all the "dis" words, feeling lost and purposeless, and sick with this cold. My journaling has been pretty sparse as well. Somehow I've been unwilling to continue whining to God even though He knows how I feel. Still when I see it written down, I sense an ungrateful spirit which seems alien to my usual joyfulness. I simply don't feel like myself.

But my God is waiting at the corners of my mind, and shows Himself when I really pause to consider Him. I was reading in the book of Ezra this week. Ezra--teacher, scribe, man of God-- in the middle of his penitent prayer says, "And now for a little while, grace has been shown from the LORD our God, to leave us a remnant to escape and to give us a peg in His holy place, that our God may enlighten our eyes and give us a measure of revival in our bondage." Ezra 9:8.

A brief background to the passage. Ezra's people (Israel) were in captivity, in bondage to a foreign nation. They were disobedient and yet Ezra was tasked to take a remnant back to their land and begin rebuilding the temple. Grace isn't mentioned often in the Old Testament, so it grabbed my attention. As I read further my mind resonated with "a peg in His Holy place," which to me means to be *fastened* and secure.

Thus we see our eyes can be enlightened, and--here is what I hung on to--"to give us (me) a measure of revival in our (my) bondage." I'm feeling in bondage to disillusionment and disappointment, I so needed that promised "measure of revival." Although I may still struggle emotionally with the "dis" feelings my mind is fixed, as a peg in a sure place, *fastened* on the truth of God's grace extended to me. He still draws me to himself no matter what is going on inside me — failure to stay close to Him or various forms of disobedience. And I am sensing the urge to return. "Revive me, O LORD, for Your name's sake! For Your righteousness' sake bring my soul out of trouble." Psalm 143:11. Revived and **FASTENED**. A signpost to be celebrated.

There. I think I feel better. Just typing the words of truth has uplifted me. May I offer the same to you? Wherever you are, whatever your circumstances in this moment, God is present, and His grace-filled voice is calling your name. Will you answer Him with me? Let's let our hearts and minds be *fastened* on Him and His truth.

Thank you for the opportunity you offer me to share my heart with you.

HEART MEDITATIONS

Hallelujah! A good report, health-wise. The cold is nearly gone, and I am not suffering with the gout anymore. I'm so grateful. Feeling good is wonderful! Thank you for partnering with me with your prayers and sweet caring. They mean the world to me.

It was a good week. We took a speaking trip to Oregon which was wonderful, and I appreciate your prayers for the events. I was so warmly welcomed and I enjoyed each event. I consider it an honor to be invited to speak the truth of the Gospel and get to know women who are working so hard to bring about these luncheons. Additionally, we were privileged to spend time with friends--totally enjoyable, sweet fellowship. All in all, it's been a wonderful few days.

I mentioned above how honored I feel to speak at events that express God's love and message of salvation. But as I pondered this after we got home, it occurred to me that although I enjoy the speaking, it is imperative that I stay connected with the Source of all truth. The words I speak should come straight from God's heart. As it says in John 3:30, "He must increase, and I must decrease." It's easy, when someone gives a talks over and over, to think that they have it down pat, but I never want to get to that place of complacency and lose the sense of wonder and privilege that carrying the Word of God brings.

So I was writing in my journal how much I longed for the words that I speak to have substance and not fluff. As so often happens, God had a word especially for me. I turned to my devotional passage for the day and found it to be Psalm 19:14, "May the words of my mouth and the meditation of my heart be acceptable in Your sight, O Lord, my Strength and my Redeemer."

Actually I have that verse on a wall hanging in my house,

and pass by those words daily. Now I will perhaps really *see* them. The words I speak must come from the meditations in my heart. Words have the power of life or death, so it's up to me to be sure they are honoring to my God: not only as I speak publicly, but in my relationships as well. It is something we all need to watch out for, I believe.

Again, I am thankful for so many things, and you all top the list. And I am grateful for the reminder to consider always my **HEART MEDITATIONS**. That should be a signpost every week, don't you think?

WORDS

Hello! It has been a pretty good week for me. I tried water aerobics, and it felt so good to be normal again. The gout pain kicked in afterward, but it's diminishing quickly. Thank You, God.

Last week I talked about Psalm 19:14--the words of my mouth and the meditations of my heart. It seems that everywhere I looked this week, there was some reference to that subject. I wasn't consciously seeking them out, but verses popped up that brought my mind back to how the words I speak can, and do, affect others. For instance, Proverbs 22:11, "He (she) who loves purity of heart and has grace on his (her) lips, the king will be his (her) friend." Oh how I want that to be true of me: a woman with grace on her lips. It is a convicting passage, as I realize how often my words are cutting, mean, and negative.

Grace on a person's lips has far-reaching results...even to the point of influencing those in power. We too easily forget that, and yield to our personal hurt feelings, or a sense of lacking worthiness. Another Proverbs verse, chapter 21:23, struck me as well, "Whoever guards his mouth and tongue keeps his soul from troubles."

As if those were not enough, I was privileged to sing on the worship team at church on Sunday, and we closed the service with *Take My Life and Let It Be*, a familiar hymn to many of us. Standing in front of the congregation to lead worship is an honor, and I don't take it lightly. Words poured out of my mouth and I prayed that they would truly be from my heart, these verses especially: "Take my voice and let me sing, always only for my King. Take my lips and let them be, filled with messages from Thee."xxx After singing, I was filled with resolve to watch my heart and my words, and then the enemy struck! An email from a family member was all it took to fill me with anger and hurt. I let thoughtless words bring me back to letting the feelings of worthlessness and envy fill the spaces of my heart instead of the grace that I had resolved to emulate.

For the past few days I have struggled with this, trying not to allow myself to descend to the level of defeated unworthiness that paralyzes me and keeps me from enjoying my relationship with my Heavenly Father, and accepting His favor.

But this morning I chanced upon Proverbs 25:11, "A word fitly spoken is like apples of gold in settings of silver." Patsy Clairmont, of Women of Faith, writes on this subject, "Some words, like a poorly-fitting shoe, pinch, cause discomfort and blister our self-esteem. But a gracious word comforts our minds and emotions like an old pair of house slippers on work-weary feet."[xxxi]

God reached out to me with the knowledge that I had let a few words, carelessly spoken, destroy all of the gracious words I had received earlier in the week. Not only the words received from other people, but the words He had spoken into my heart-- His love for me, His care of me, and His promises that wrap me in hope and delight. I had to repent, and thus receive words of grace. Words of grace that I trust will characterize my actions and reactions to those with whom I am in relationship. May I encourage you all to do the same? His Word brings salve to wounded hearts and teaches us to guard our lips. I'm trusting that my words are graciously spoken and graciously received. No wonder I chose **WORDS** as my signpost.

CELEBRATING LIFE

Greetings! The weather is HOT, and it will get worse I'm afraid. I sort of wilt in the heat, so am dreading the next few weeks. As nice as it is to have sunshine, it has its down side, at least for me.

We have been with our granddaughter this week and I have had a lot of time to do some ruminating, going over back pages in my journal, searching the scripture, and attempting to determine where I am headed next in my purpose and ministry. As I was paging through my Bible I saw a highlighted and underlined verse, Romans 6:11, and recalled that my "One Perfect Word" for the previous year was ALIVE. "Likewise you also, reckon yourselves to be dead indeed to sin, but alive to God in Christ Jesus our Lord." Not realizing at the onset of 2014 how that word would impact my life, I had to stop and thank God that yes, I am alive! Physically alive, because of the heart surgery but even better, alive in Jesus, because of His sacrifice. It is a cause for rejoicing and an impetus to live that way--moving toward healing and embracing my alive-ness.

A large part of this year, I have been struggling with feelings of defeat and despair, as you all know, if you've been following my column, surely because of some of the fallout from the recovery process. But I'm tired of it. Tired of feeling, acting, and being tired, experiencing listlessness and lethargy, excusing it with every known and contrived reason I can come up with to soothe myself. Yesterday I wrote in my journal, "Time for it to end." I had no idea what would occur later in the day.

Fred and I had decided we wanted to visit Multnomah Falls near Portland. For the past few days the gout had made me almost crippled, so I wasn't sure just how much walking I could do, but decided to try. It is a quarter mile hike up to the Bridge where you can see the falls better, and I thought, "Can I do a quarter of a mile? And almost straight up?" Thinking "a step at a time," I kept going and I made it. My feet tolerated the climb, and my spirit exulted in it. I felt alive for the first time in months, and so grateful! The trees were so green, the rushing waterfall was music to my ears, the sun warmed me, and the shade along the path was also welcome.

Yes, *alive*! Sensing sights and sounds I had only been watching from my window, in a sense. I was thinking as I headed back down the mountain how easy it is to simply sit, and watch life go by, contriving excuses to keep from engaging, and how marvelous it is to find yourself seeing, tasting, feeling, and yes, walking.

I am celebrating today, and pray that you will join me in a song of joy to our Creator. Praise His holy Name. "Let everything that has breath, praise the LORD. Praise the LORD!" Psalm 150:6

CELEBRATING LIFE. I'm rejoicing in my signpost this week, using every breath to praise my God.

KNEADING

I'm going to do something a little different today. It's been kind of a tough week, so I'm asking for your prayers. But rather than complain and gripe, I decided to look through some of the meditations I have written in the past to find something that would grab your attention, as well as mine. Sometimes I enjoy looking back and reading some of my old poetry, remembering how God had met me and to reflect on incidents where I could really hear Him speaking to my heart. I found this one, "I Need To Be Kneaded," that I wrote after my precious mother-in-law had tried to teach me to make bread--although I never did master that skill.

But as I read it, I thought, "This is where I am right now--again!" And so I post it today, trying to understand my present situation, and hoping that if you find yourself in a similar circumstance when nothing seems to be going right, you may be reminded of how our Heavenly Father's hands stay poised to work on us as we yield to His tender touch.

I NEED TO BE KNEADED
"For it is God who works in you both to will and to do for His good pleasure." Philippians 2:13

A mound of dough, a floured board.
I am learning to make bread.
It's a first for me--the working of the dough
beneath my hands.
I am amazed at the response;
the more I push,
the more it springs back.

My mother says,
"The more you knead, the better it likes it."
So I think, Father, I'm rather like a mound of dough
lying on a floured board under Your hands.
You're kneading me, and how do I respond?

Just as my kneading helps activate the yeast,
making good bread;
God, may Your working on me activate the Spirit life
you've placed in me.
Help me to understand
that to serve You well,
I need to be kneaded.

God's **KNEADING** in my life, His working on me, is so very important to my spiritual well-being. I so often resist it, but am reminded today that in yielding my spirit is activated. I am, as always, grateful for the precious Word of God. So, Father, prepare me to grow with Your tender kneading.

COMFORT

What a beautiful morning. I love the coolness and sweetness of an early summer day--like a blessing poured over my soul. How wonderful is our Creator.

Thanks for stopping here for a few minutes. I always appreciate those of you who comment, but I know there are many who are reading who don't. I surely appreciate each one who pauses to read my words.

It's the middle of a busy week. My husband says it's either feast or famine; either nothing is going on, or everything happens at once. There are a lot of pleasurable events, errands and things to accomplish in the next few days. Even as I write this I am aware of those whose lives aren't pleasurable right now, and I offer my prayers and hope for you.

With that in mind, I have been going through my Bible looking at passages about grace, and on Monday I was so blessed to read these words: "Seeing then that we have a great High Priest who has passed through the heavens, Jesus the Son of God, let us hold fast our confession. For we do not have a High Priest who cannot sympathize with our weaknesses, but was in all points tempted as we are, yet without sin. Let us therefore come boldly to the throne of grace, that we may obtain mercy and find grace to help in time of need." Hebrews 4:14-16.

Before that day was over I had received four telephone calls from friends whose lives were in turmoil and were in need of these comforting words from Scripture, as I was myself. It was so good to share with hurting ones that God who sits on the Throne of Grace has an abundant supply of mercy and grace, and gives them freely--we need only to come.

I think that the overriding thought for my signpost today is **COMFORT.** Only God can provide just the comfort we need.

114

Perhaps you find a need for this comfort this morning. I pray you will come boldly and avail yourself of the limitless resources from your Heavenly Father. He longs to touch your life with a new realization of what He offers you--mercy and grace to help in time of need. Just come.

I pray rich blessings in your life today and always.

WATER

Summer is here in earnest, and we are being cautioned about the possibility of drought and told to be careful in our use of water. Even while other parts of the country are fighting flooding. It's too bad we can't all share in perfect weather, or at least have a happy medium.

The last time we were in this predicament, I wrote the following.

DROUGHT
"Come, all who are thirsty, come to the water." Isaiah 55:1

Dusty automobiles, dried-up lawns,
flowers wilting in the heat.
There's a water shortage.
The abundance to which we've become accustomed
is suddenly rationed.
We are in a drought, and it is irritating
to feel ourselves deprived.
How wasteful I've been, considering the supply endless.
Now, mourning the lack,
I am chagrined to realize all I've taken for granted.

But what about my spiritual drought?
I can't complain about using up
the Living Water available to me;
it's Source is unending, yet I don't partake
from its fountain nearly as freely
as I have drawn from the faucet of earthly water,
which is running dry.

I need both to survive.

But I must conserve the one and gulp the other.

How incredible to realize that

the water that fills my eternal spirit

flows unceasingly from the Fountain of Life

and will never lead to a drought.

I have been reading and pondering the 3rd Chapter of Proverbs for many days. Filling my own spiritual dryness from its refreshing, though challenging, wisdom. Next week I want to examine some of what I have learned from digging into what I had only planned to read through lightly. My goal was to read a chapter of Proverbs a day, but I simply couldn't get past this chapter and I am so excited to share it with you.

Until then, know that your prayers have been effective: the gout and accompanying pain is disappearing every day and I have begun to do some walking around the neighborhood in an attempt to reclaim some of the heart-healthy behaviors I lost with the onset of gout and the flu months ago. Thank you for praying for me. I so appreciate it.

Maybe you would want to delve into the riches of Proverbs 3 along with me? Join me here and we will explore what wisdom really is.

Blessings to you all.

NECKLACE

Welcome, my readers! Last week I challenged you to look at Proverbs 3. It has been a real treat for me to examine it over the past couple of weeks and I also promised to share some of what I have learned. It begins thus: "My son (daughter) do not forget my law, but let your heart keep my commands; for length of days and long life and peace they will add to you. Let not mercy and truth forsake you. Bind them around your neck, write them on the tablet of your heart, and so find favor and high esteem in the sight of God and man." Proverbs 3:1-4

These verses are here as guidance from a father to a son, or daughter, in my case. When pondering scripture I often find it helpful to look for lists. In these verses I discovered a list of instructions and then, a list of the resulting benefits. The instructions are 1) don't forget his law, 2) keep his commands, 3) don't let mercy and truth forsake you, 4) bind them around your neck, and 5) write them on the tablet of your heart. Pretty straightforward.

The results include 1) length of days and long life, 2) peace, 3) favor and high esteem in the sight of God and man.

Peace and length of days are the results of obedience. Taking hold of mercy and truth brings high esteem and favor of **both** God and man. The wisdom of obedience is the thrust of this passage. What is so fascinating to me is the instruction to take mercy and truth and wear them as a necklace, so to speak--an *outward* reminder of how to live. And then to write them on the tablet of our hearts--an *inward* motivation or reminder to live in a way that brings us high esteem and favor from both God and man. That is the longing of my heart. How about yours?

I wrote in my journal, "Maybe I should have a necklace that has Mercy and Truth engraved on it. Of course, it's an inner attitude and awareness more than a real piece of jewelry. But how great it would be to have a constant reminder of the way a wise woman lives, reacts and is motivated.

Well, unbeknownst to me, Fred had ordered a necklace for me as a gift--just an "I love you," I guess. It doesn't say "mercy and truth," but it is called "God's Heart" and is beautiful, with the name of God stylized into a heart and bright stones spelling out the "O" in the middle. When I wear it I am reminded of these precious Proverbs verses that have come to mean so much to me, and my gratitude knows no bounds. Fred had no idea of what was going on in my mind and in my journal, but God did. He gave me a signpost to wear: a **NECKLACE**, an outward reminder of the mercy and truth that characterize His love for me.

Well, that's only the first four verses. There's so much more, but I will wait until next week for another installment. I'd welcome you to join me.

WISDOM

In my last thoughts I challenged you to look at Proverbs 3 in some depth. I found in verses 13-26 a touching tribute to wisdom, describing the benefits of finding "her." It's interesting that the metaphor of a woman is used for wisdom isn't it?

Here is a list of wisdom's gifts (paraphrased) that I culled from these verses:

1) The gains are better than gold and silver;
2) More precious than rubies;
3) Can't be compared with all the things one could desire;
4) Length of days;
5) Riches and honor;
6) Pleasant ways;
7) Peaceful paths;
8) A tree of life;
9) Happiness;
10) Life to your soul;
11) Grace to your neck;
12) Safety in walking;
13) Sweet sleep with no fear;
14) No fear of sudden terror, or trouble from the wicked.

"For the LORD will be your confidence and will keep your foot from being caught." Proverbs 3:26

Wisdom, true wisdom, is of great benefit and blessing when it is attained and retained. It is worth seeking. It's more, I think, than simply *hearing* the right words from God as counsel. It is a way of living, of thinking and reacting. Charles Spurgeon, that great preacher of old once said, "Wisdom, I suppose, is the right use of knowledge."[xxxii] Ponder on the above list this week and perhaps you can come up with more. I have surely been blessed.

One more thing. We have been invited by our son to spend a week at Malibu, the Young Life camp in British Columbia. This place has been pivotal in my walk with Jesus and we are incredibly blessed to be going back. It is a gift, in part, to celebrate our 50th anniversary. We are leaving Saturday, and I would ask for your prayers as we go, specifically that God can use us to minister to the military families who'll be guests as well and that we will shine for Him. Also for our son Kent, as he is the camp speaker, and will need much prayer to undergird him as he shares, in his inimitable way, the sweetness of the Gospel message. Needless to say, I am "twitter-pated" at the prospect of what is ahead for us next week.

Hopefully I'll be able to post at some point next week to let you share in what God is doing. But if not, know that we will be depending on your prayer support. And we will tell you all about it when we get home. Thank you all, and may God bless each of you richly.

CONNECTIONS

Joyful greetings! I trust all is well with you. But whatever is going on in your life, let's be reminded that the scripture tells us to be joyful, and that joy comes from Jesus.

I was unable to post a column last week, tucked away as we were in the wilds of British Columbia at Young Life's Malibu Club. No phones, no TV, no Internet. It was good to get away from all that and focus on what is really important. I came across a quote from Richard Halverson, former Chaplain of the U.S. Senate. He writes, following a family visit to Malibu, "An unforgettable experience with indescribable scenery and accommodations. I have known of Young Life's ministry throughout the years and I know of no more effective ministry in reaching teenagers for Christ."[xxxiii] How I agree.

Fred and I have been privileged to attend Malibu a few times in the past as adult campers. I also had the opportunity to be a counselor for high school girls one summer, but this past week was something different. It was Military Families Week, an effort to give back to those who have given so much to serve our country. Instead of 325 teenagers romping about laughing and learning, the place was filled with moms and dads and children (from babies to teenagers) bonding with each other. What joy it was to watch daddies actually spending time with their kids, acting goofy, dancing with their wives, and best of all, sitting quietly to hear the message of God's incredible love for them. I am forever changed.

I am humbly grateful it was our son, Kent, who stood on the platform and shared the clear and potent truth of the Gospel. He is a marvelous communicator and has such a passion for telling people about Jesus. Everyone enjoyed him, laughed with him, and connected with his message. We were privileged to be Small

Group Leaders and had four precious families with whom WE connected. Now I am musing on the many different **CONNECTIONS** formed, making it my signpost for the week.

As I've spent some time thinking about the people in our lives, I am touched so deeply to consider how wonderful it is to explore with joy and thanksgiving the connections God sends our way. 1 Corinthians 12 talks a lot about the body of Christ and how we are all individuals, but yet a part of something so much greater. "For as the body is one and has many members, but all the members of that one body, being many, are one body, so also is Christ." 1 Corinthians 12:12. I also rejoice to read Verse 18, "But now God has set the members, each one of them, in the body just as He pleased." These connections, these relationships, are not by accident, and I am very grateful for what He has pleased to do for us.

It was at Malibu that God began pulling me back to Himself, almost 30 years ago--so Malibu has a real emotional attachment that brought back many memories. I will forever be grateful for this gift of our week away. I have basked once more in the beauty of God's creation, have been reminded of His love, mercy and compassion to me, and have grasped His hand ever more tightly in response to that tenderness that covers me.

Plus, I got a real workout physically, and my legs are much stronger than when I left home. Stiff and hurting, yes, but so thankful that I am healthy enough to have done what I did. Thanks for standing with me over this journey of the past months. May God touch your lives with the richness of His love as you continue your own journey.

MEMORIES

Good Morning. The first thing I want to say is how sweet it has been to receive all the good wishes sent to us to celebrate our 50th anniversary. It has been incredible to read the greetings both from people who have been a longstanding part of our lives and from new friends. We have been overjoyed and filled with precious memories.

I think that's what I want to talk about this morning. My signpost for this week: **MEMORIES.** What a huge part in life they play. Good and bad, they are what make up our past, color our present day, and hopefully bring direction to our future.

What struck me as I was pondering earlier is how completely God dwells in the center of my memories. Often when I look back, I see darkness, sadness and grief, but there is also the sense that my Heavenly Father was with me in it. I can see that as I look back now, even though I couldn't at the time.

When my mother died of polio, I was nine years old. We were living in a tiny town in Wyoming, a small enough place that all the kids in town ran around together. There are such wonderful memories of the things we did, the fun we had. It's amazing to me, that when I think of that town, what resonates is not the grief from losing Mother. I believe God's mercy covers the pain with joyful reminders in order for me to look into the loss with a heart that is healing; healing because of the knowledge of His presence. He was there. He is here, now.

Searching through my Bible to find references to memories, I looked up Isaiah 43, a chapter that has meant so much to me. In verses 18 and 19 it reads, "Forget the former things; do not dwell on the past. See, I am doing a new thing! Now it springs up; do you not perceive it? I am making a way in the desert and streams in the wasteland."

Even though it says to forget the former things, I believe it means not to hang your hat there. We can't *forget*--our memories are part of us, but we can keep ourselves looking forward in hope at the new thing God promises. This passage jumped out at me today and couldn't be ignored.

I have been in a valley for quite a while, as you know, feeling low and not quite myself, but I need to say that I am renewed in my spirit, reading that God is all about doing something new--in me. He is taking my past, my memories, and breathing on them, forming a beautiful and useful stream in my desert.

I am getting excited! And I am glad that you all are taking this journey with me. Punch your ticket. All aboard. See you at the next stop!

SHARING

Greetings. It is good to sit down and write some thoughts to share with you.

Last night I had the opportunity to speak at a little country church nearby for a women's gathering, which was an amazing experience. As I began telling my story, I noticed three women on the first row weeping and comforting each other. Wondering if I had touched a nerve or upset someone, I sent up a quick prayer for guidance and kept on, giving my testimony and reading some of my poetry. Afterward, these women met me in the aisle and I learned that they, too, had lost their mother to polio when they were small children, and their lives in many ways paralleled mine. Their last glimpse of their mother, like mine, was in an iron lung. It was no wonder that they were weeping with their memories.

They told me they had never before met someone who could completely understand, who had gone through circumstances nearly identical to theirs--but of course, neither had I. Sharing my life, my testimony, had moved them and helped them to see some things from a different perspective.

Can you comprehend the joy this brought to me? To know God brought me there, moved in my life in a way that could impact others, and gave me the awesome opportunity of sharing. This is my signpost for this week: **SHARING**. How wonderful it is to look into someone's eyes and see such empathy and understanding. I am so excited this morning and grateful to share this with you. Because I know many of you were praying, and when you see your prayers answered in such a dramatic way, it is sure to bless you. And I bless you, too, for your faithfulness in prayer and support for whatever ministry God places before me. I love you all.

I close with these verses from Psalm 78:2a, 6-7, which

explain how God uses us to carry His word to those that come after. "I will open my mouth in a parable; that the generation to come might know them, the children who would be born; that they may arise and declare them to their children, that they might set their hope in God, and not forget the works of God, but keep his commandments." It reminds me that, even though my mother was taken so early, her influence (and her prayers) continue in my life as I commit to walk with my God.

THE RIGHT TURN

Well, it's a new day, with adventure awaiting. I sit here praying that there is peace and hope in your lives. This past week we have had several messages from other loved ones about pain, loss and medical crises in their lives. I am reminded over and over again of the brevity of life, how we are not promised an easy road, but that reminder is balanced by the wonder of hope for all who trust in Christ. My heart settles into the knowledge of that rock-solid hope, reminding us all of the truth of the Gospel, and this is not all there is.

We got lost yesterday as we were trying to find the home of an old friend. To me, there is nothing more frustrating than not knowing how to get where you want to go. Tension was thick in the car. I felt guilty because apparently I had written the directions wrong (this happens a lot lately), and Fred was becoming more and more anxious as we got farther and farther from our destination. You know the old saying about men never asking for directions! Well, after a lot of wasted time I asked a woman at a convenience store where we had stopped how to get to the road we wanted. We took her up on her offer to lead us there, going far out of her way, and we eventually arrived at the right place.

Obviously, there is a spiritual application here: we can become grumpy and frustrated when making all the wrong turns, unwilling to ask for help and determined to do it all ourselves. I do this in living my life, too, not just in the car. But I must humble myself and ask for the help God offers me constantly. I need not *search* — the answer is there because of His presence in my life.

However, I sometimes prefer to fume and fret and cry tears of anxiousness. Hence, I am chagrined to announce my signpost for this week: **THE RIGHT TURN**. What relief when a sweet stranger, an off-duty nurse by the way, took the time to lead us and we discovered what we had been seeking.

It reminds me of a wonderful promise from Jeremiah 29:13-14. "And you will seek Me and find Me, when you search for Me with all your heart. I will be found by you' says the LORD, 'and I will bring you back from your captivity; I will gather you from all the nations and from all the places where I have driven you,' says the LORD, 'and I will bring you to the place from which I cause you to be carried away.'" Carried away and captives in faraway places, God never forgets His children. He *will* be found, we just need to avail ourselves of that promise.

What relief occurs when we submit to God's leading and find once more the right turn He has laid out for us. Again, it challenged me to be sensitive to someone else who is lost and needs assistance or an encouraging word. I hope I remember this. And I am grateful: many of you have taken the time to encourage me and offer guidance. Please know you are appreciated.

Keep your eyes and heart open today. Perhaps you will find someone who is lost or confused, one to whom God is leading you so you can bring the aid of your presence, your support and a hand to hold--helping someone find **THE RIGHT TURN.** Isn't that a great signpost for this week?

I will be looking too.

TOTAL RECALL

Hello from the road. We've been busy on a journey visiting friends, and sometimes I get so overwhelmed that my mind goes blank (I hear some of you laughing) and my thoughts are jumbled, so much so that I can't seem to come up with a subject to write about. Earlier I wrote about memories and how important they are to us--both the good ones and the bad ones. I really enjoy meeting up with people who I haven't seen for many years, cherishing the instant of recognition, and the "Oh, yes, I remember you!" moment. I also enjoy making new friends, new contacts that promise a host of new memories.

I've been considering all the times that God tells us in scripture that He remembers us. Often that word remember is a translation that means "to reflect upon," more than to "call to mind." So, as I sit and reminisce with old friends and family, it is interesting to see the different ways that we recall certain incidents. My recollections and their recollections often are completely different. My mind remembers one piece of an incident and it may stick out in my mind, yet has been totally forgotten by the other person. Conversely, their memory contains a part that I am sure really happened, but which I cannot recollect at all! I am also sure that it isn't *all* from old age!

So, isn't it reassuring that our Heavenly Father has **TOTAL RECALL?** That there isn't *one* thing about us that He has forgotten about us? That He never will abandon us to our mistakes nor our faulty recall of His blessings toward us? That He *is* truth and He knows us inside and out, all the while loving us and delighting in the completeness of His design of us? And we have His promise that He will "never leave us nor forsake us." Hebrews 13:5.

As I close for this week, looking forward to the days ahead, I hope that you will be rejoicing in the good memories that are part of your life. Trust the not-so-good ones to Him too, knowing His **TOTAL RECALL** and His grace might cover them with a quilt of His love.

JOURNEY MERCIES

We have been traveling, as you know, seeking to celebrate our 50th anniversary. God has blessed us so much with memories and re-connections. You've likely noticed how often I've commented here on the excitement we have experienced along the way. Also we have known lovely weather and safety on the roads and freeways. There have been a few close calls, causing Fred frustration with those *crazy idiot drivers*...but thankfully angels ride on all four corners of our Subaru and we are extremely grateful. **JOURNEY MERCIES** seems an appropriate signpost for our trip. I often meditate on Psalm 91:11, "For He shall give His angels charge over you to keep you in all of your ways." Yes, please!

We are often reminded of God's promises as we travel, not only of protection, but joyful times of refreshing that come from being in the presence of old friends and enjoying sweet fellowship with new ones. We do have great joy and consolation from the wonderful welcomes, gracious hospitality and loving arms with which we have been greeted. In addition to the joy this brings, it affirms our marriage and that God has allowed us to be part of the lives of so many--friends and family alike.

Thank you for your prayers as we journey on. Again, I am struggling with hip pain that has been distressing. Unfortunately it has kept us from doing a lot of what we had planned. Fred has been wonderful to me, so kind and helpful. I appreciate his care for me so very much. I am anxious though to find relief somehow, so prayers for that are appreciated. Thank you.

WHIRLWIND

Well, I must say, this trip so far has been quite a **WHIRLWIND**. I am using that as my signpost for this week. Or maybe I should say "this time period" because posting here has not been a weekly event. All my attention has been upon the traveling and the places, celebrating the people that are a part of it. Someone once penned this comment, "The best things in life are the places we have been, the people we have met, and the memories we have made along the way." I am so grateful to say that this is totally true in our lives. This nostalgia tour has brought us back into those places where memories were made, and we are reconnecting and recollecting. However, my journaling has taken a back seat. We are in one place or another for such a short time, thus, the focus is not on reading my Bible and contemplating God's words. I am loathe to admit this, but it is true. I always plan to write in the car, but there are too many distractions. We have traveled to Wyoming, South Dakota, Iowa, Wisconsin, Ontario Canada, New York, Connecticut, and now Maryland (plus all the states in between). Yes, a whirlwind. And we're only halfway through our planned trip. It's exciting and gratifying and I'm loving it but, at the same time, missing my usual time communicating with God.

When I thought about using **WHIRLWIND** for my signpost today, I looked up the scripture from Job 38:1, "Then the LORD answered Job out of the whirlwind." God can speak to us even when our circumstances seem like a whirlwind. Job's comforters had just mentioned that they could not find the Almighty, but God heard that complaint and responded with an answer.

In 1 Kings 19:11-12 the prophet Elijah also hears God speaking to him. "Then He said, 'Go out, and stand on the mountain before the LORD.' And behold the LORD passed by, and a great and strong wind tore into the mountains and broke the rocks in pieces before the LORD, but the LORD was not in the wind; and after the wind an earthquake, but the LORD was not in the earthquake; and after the earthquake a fire, but the LORD was not in the fire; and after the fire a still small voice." Since I realize that He is speaking to me, I am chagrined about not listening lately. I'm focusing more attention to what is going on around me than I am on hearing. And I am bereft.

The whirlwind is enjoyable though, I am discovering: the cacophony of precious voices, the hurry, and the stop and go. How much more enjoyable, however, if I can keep my heart attuned to that still small voice. It is made even more precious by the outward signs of His love in the memories and experiences.

DISTANCE

We are home: 9300 miles, 32 states, many different beds! Incredible experiences that will take some time to process. I'm relieved to be home safely, but I'm exhausted and in horrible pain. The doctor gave me a cortisone injection and prescribed pain meds which are finally giving me a bit of relief. There is so much to do after returning from a long trip, and I don't feel up to dealing with *any* of it. The need to restore my strength tops the list so I am grateful for a little lessening of the pain.

However, the most urgent thing facing me as I return is the distance between God and me. I have allowed this to happen by putting my time with Him on hold, trying instead to get through the trip, while bearing the pain in my hip. The knowledge that He loves me--even though I pulled away and have been angry with Him--is what I must hold closely. I've missed the feeling of my Bible in my hands, finding some perverse satisfaction in ignoring Him, when He's been so gracious. I am asking His forgiveness for so many of my thoughts and actions that have doused cold water on the warmth of intimacy with Him, bringing a sense of loss in my soul. I so need His promised mercy.

I turn to Him beginning with gratitude--for all those miles of safety on the road, protection from storms and hurricanes, and loving arms that greeted us wherever we visited. Above all, Fred's overarching, constant support and comfort--his unending strength and patience. And gratitude for God's protection, because we may never know how His unseen, unnoticed blessings fell under our radar. Though we will never know, we are thankful for each one.

In Jeremiah 23:23-24 God asks a poignant question. "'Am I a God near at hand, and not a God afar off? Can anyone hide himself in secret places so I shall not see him?' says the LORD. 'Do

I not fill heaven and earth?'" Yes, He *is* near at hand and no, I cannot hide from Him. When I focus my eyes on that truth, the distance fades and His loving presence makes itself sweetly evident. So while I am naming **DISTANCE** as my signpost for this week, I am filled with praise that it is not a permanent condition. May each of you draw near to the God who promises His *nearness* in the days ahead. I certainly will be.

WHINING

Greetings. This is going to be a hard one to write. The pain relief didn't last very long so I was referred to an orthopedic surgeon, and I am scheduled for a total hip replacement as soon as possible. He said I'm bone-on-bone, and I guess that's why it hurts so badly.

I'm exhausted from fighting the pain and can't seem to concentrate. Anywhere I sit down, I immediately fall asleep. There's an irony here. My blog was intended to be an encouragement for all of us so that we can share God's working in our lives. Right now I have nothing left with which to encourage you. We have often walked through hard places together. Now I'm acknowledging how much I need you to come alongside me with your prayers and encouragement.

I realize that on the other side of the surgery will be an end to the pain of the past few years, but still I'm terrified, and don't know why. I can't seem to settle into a calm and trusting mode, and everything is suffering--my relationship with God, for example. I'm irritable, so pray for Fred! Right now, with another physical bump in the road, God sort of feels far away. It seems as though it has been a year of my rear end being glued to the recliner.

Sorry, I know this is a whiny note. And I must tell you about another wrinkle in our lives. Fred has been diagnosed with bladder cancer and he has to have surgery immediately. So do I. Thus we have to decide who goes first; who will be best able to nurse the other one. Confusion reigns. The holidays are approaching as well, and we feel a bit blindsided by the necessity of making major decisions and leaning on medical advice.

In the meantime, I've been clinging to John 16:33, "These things I have spoken to you, that in Me you may have peace. In the world you will have tribulation, but be of good cheer; I have overcome the world." It's a good promise to absorb, one that neutralizes the poisonous weekly signpost: **WHINING.**

SILENCE

Well, I guess the whining continues. As I consider the need for surgery, my mood swings from discouragement to hopefulness depending on how much I have to walk and how horrible I feel (not to mention how fearful I am).

The doctor prescribed Percocet for me as well, which makes me sleepy and disoriented and I can't drive while taking it, understandably. But with a little lessening of pain, my spirits are higher. Still I am so tired of all this.

I am not a huge believer in simply flipping open my Bible to receive *words* but this morning I did it, because I did not have a clue as to where to turn. Thankfully I just *happened upon* Psalm 62, which is heavily underlined and highlighted, finding these precious observations once more. They are seriously uplifting me this morning: "My soul, wait silently for God alone, for my expectation is from Him. He only is my rock and my salvation; He is my defense; I shall not be moved. In God is my salvation and my glory; the rock of my strength, and my refuge, is in God." Psalm 62:5-7

As I read and pondered I was reminded of the lyrics to a praise chorus that's titled "Word of God, Speak."[xxxiv] And I thought to myself, what I need is not necessarily to be heard, but to hear what God would say. Speak to me, Lord. In Psalm 46:10 I hear this instruction: "Be still and know that I am God." Oh, how I've been complaining to Him, not paying attention to what He might be saying. Now I recognize the need for my signpost for the week: **SILENCE.** Again I hear the lyrics in my mind, "please let me stay and rest in Your holiness. Word of God, speak."[xxxv]

God's words are precious, necessary food for my soul. If you hear nothing else from me through these weeks, hear *that.* And let's spend some time listening…in the **SILENCE.**

INTERRUPTION

Hi! I keep wanting to tell you all about our trip around the USA, but I find that a different journey seems more important to share this week.

We have had another bump in the health road. I had been sick for several days, nauseated and all the rest that goes with it. I think the pain medication was the cause. I didn't drink enough water, apparently, and got dehydrated. On Sunday morning when I woke up, I couldn't speak coherently. I couldn't make a bit of sense, even though in my mind I was speaking the right words. Neither could I write anything but gibberish on paper. Fred called 911 and they carted me off in an ambulance.

What had occurred was what the doctors diagnosed as a TIA, which can be a precursor to a stroke--some even call it a mild stroke. As soon as they pumped in IV fluids, I began to come out of it, starting to speak sentences that made sense. All the symptoms--dysphasia and hallucinations, have cleared and all the tests showed no visible cause for the TIA. After three days in the hospital and many tests, I'm now home and feeling pretty well. I am advised to seek out a neurologist to go over the tests, etc., to see if they can find anything.

In the meantime, I'm waiting, too, for clearance for my scheduled hip replacement surgery. My doctors are uneasy about putting me under anesthesia, so they all have to clear me, and I can't see them for a few days.

So, there I am. Everything has changed and I am working to comprehend just what it all means. I'll be exploring it together with you over the next few weeks. I cannot describe the terror of not being able to speak, nor use words to communicate. For me, as a writer and speaker, it was earth-shaking.

I admit I was pretty much out of it, so that I wasn't aware

of the implications until I got home and looked at the paper on which I had tried to write. I was stunned. But Fred had been aware, and he was terrified. I haven't fully taken it in, but I know God has a lesson for me and I am excited to discover what it is.

Sometimes these lessons are hard to learn, but I did finally find and apply the truth of Proverbs 16:9. "A man's heart plans his way, but the LORD directs his steps."

I suddenly realize how important being a writer has been to me, and now I see that it can be taken away in a heartbeat. The first morning home from the hospital I wrote the following prayer to God. It's not completely developed, but it expresses some of what is going on in my heart:

> "You took Your words away from me
>> So I could see
> Just what a tabernacle
>> I had let them build in me;
> And then, in gracious, compassionate love,
>> You trustingly gave them back to me."

My friends, I am blessed. I see the past few days as an **INTERRUPTION**, and thus I am making that my signpost. I'm praying that you will continue to accompany me on this path that lies ahead. Next time I hope to have news about the new hip waiting for me.

DROUGHT

Progress report. I'm still struggling to express in writing all that is happening inside me, but I'm going to give it a try. We know that Fred's surgical procedure will be first, so when that is over we'll be able to relax in one area.

I do have to tell you that even without the pain medication which was making me sick, the pain has been bearable, and I give credit to God for that. I am doing very little moving around and I have a cane and a walker, so I'm not stressing like I was, but I'm so very grateful for the lessening of pain. That's the medical report.

I promised to share with you some of the things I have learned/am learning from my experience with what I was told was a TIA, a minor stroke. It has changed so much within me, things that I have not yet begun to examine. But there is one illustration I need to describe for you. Dehydration, lack of water, created a tempest in my body. One result was a malfunction in my brain. Terrifyingly scary but easy to resolve, as I mentioned last time. To us it was miraculous, God-ordained and God- performed.

The other dimension has not been lost on me, however. I was *spiritually* dehydrated as well--having pulled away from the intimacy, journaling and Scripture meditation that normally sustain me. I allowed earthy matters: vacation, pain, travel, etc., to eclipse my usual routine. I scarcely opened my journal the whole two months we were away, and coming home to surgery (for both Fred and me) made me pull away even more. I was parched for God--knowing it, but too stubborn to do anything about it. I was not following my own advice!

When I came home from the hospital I couldn't stop weeping, so I turned to the Word of God for comfort. It was as though Living Water gushed into me, and I found Him again;

found Him, found my words, found myself. Oh, how we need that constant presence of His Word in our lives. I hope I never again let this happen, neither spiritually, nor physically. That I never allow **DROUGHT** to linger in my soul.

Is your soul dehydrated? Are you dry? Please search His Word--let Living Water nourish and hydrate your spirit. That is what I'm doing now. Will you join me? Refreshment is so sweet.

THE WAITING ROOM

Greetings. As I have been prohibited from having anesthesia until cleared by a neurologist, my hip operation has been postponed.

The decision as to who would have the first surgery was made by default: it will be Fred. The decision was actually out of our hands. I'm sitting in the **WAITING ROOM**, which is most definitely my signpost for the week. Having been the patient over the past months, this is a new experience for me. Fred is prepped, our son Kent is with me and our son Kirk has called with the encouragement of his medical expertise. Thus we are waiting. I have often thought about the subject of waiting, and all that it involves. What we need to do, as Psalm 37:7 says, is "Rest in the LORD, and wait patiently for Him." I realize, as I sit here trying to control my restlessness, that I have a long way to go before my spirit can settle into the proper kind of waiting that God sometimes asks of us.

. . .

Now I guess the surgery is over because the doctor steps into the room to advise us of the proceedings. "It is definitely cancer," he says. "The tumor was very large, but I think I got all of it." He then went on to tell us about all that can be done for a bladder cancer patient these days, including making a new bladder from the small intestine. Very comforting I'm sure, but I am numb. I don't think we truly realized the seriousness of what was going on, and I was blithely ignorant of any consequences. As the doctor left the room, tears burned in my eyes.

My son, who was also a bit blindsided, looked at me and said, "Mom, didn't we put Dad into God's hands as they wheeled him out? Now, then, this is the time when we put that into practice. Do we really trust Him?" I wanted to scream, "Of course I do!"

Then I realized that it was easy to use the word trust when it applies to someone else—but for my husband? Not so easy. Our son's words though, convicted me and I was brought to my knees in surrender. The **WAITING ROOM** had become a holy place.

Now we wait again, this time for biopsy results, and healing. But my waiting has a different flavor. I have experienced true submission to God's will, and a newfound faith is shining in my heart. I am trusting in my sovereign God, who makes my personal **WAITING ROOM** a sanctuary for His presence.

GOOD NEWS

A new chapter begins. Bringing my husband home from the hospital, hurting from the surgery, I am so grateful that our son is here with us. He stayed the first night while Fred slept in his recliner and I dozed anxiously next to him. I couldn't sleep well. The next day our son spent fielding phone calls and keeping us focused on the new reality in our lives medically, and the reality of God's presence through all that is ahead.

We thought we had to wait for ten days for the pathology report, and had steeled ourselves for the waiting to hear results, but our gracious God had another plan. Three days later the doctor called and told us that the cancer was low-grade, surface only, non-invasive and he had been able to remove it all. We just stood in the living room and shouted praise to God. Of course there will be some immuno-therapy needed, but although malignant, the tumor is gone!

As if that were not enough good news, I had visited the neurologist earlier that day and, having reviewing all the tests, he told me that I had *not* had a TIA. The symptoms were caused by kidney failure brought on by dehydration. Who knew? I had been clueless that not being able or willing to drink water could cause such a violent reaction. Aside from clearing me for the hip surgery, it put me on another emotional roller coaster. I had spent the last two weeks or so getting used to living with a stroke threat, only to discover it was not a threat at all. This surely was a wake-up call though, to be more aware of my health and the importance of drinking enough water. It is vital to every chemical reaction in our bodies. We are blessed that clean water is so easily available to us in this country. Why do we so often neglect that free gift?

It reminds me of one of the last invitations issued to us in Revelation 22:17b. "And the Spirit and the bride say, 'Come!' And let him who thirsts come. Whoever desires, let him take the water of life freely." Water, necessary for life, freely offered. May we comprehend this truth, both spiritually and physically.

There are no words to express how a reversal of emotions can bring such joy--a quick trip from the valley to the mountain top. It is little wonder I am having difficulty finding a signpost for this week other than to simply say **GOOD NEWS**! How excited I am to share this with you, and to give to God all the glory for answered prayer!

GIFTS

It is Christmas Eve. A rather strange one, to be sure. We are so gratefully blessed. Fred is much more comfortable now that the catheter is removed and we know what we are facing therapy-wise to prevent a reoccurrence of the cancer. And since he is improving rapidly, we feel he will be well able to help me when I have the upcoming hip surgery. Believe me, I am looking forward to that. The pain right now is intense, and since I can't take the normal pain meds, it's in teeth-gritting mode. Still, God is merciful and though I'm miserable, I am getting along okay.

Tomorrow is Christmas Day. At our house there are no decorations, no preparations for a big dinner and no gifts--not physical or material gifts anyway. The gifts we will be opening in the morning can only be felt with our hearts. Our love for each other, the companionship we share, the constant reassurances of the love of our children and grandchildren, medical knowledge and the healing hand of our Great Physician. These are the valuable things for which we will be praising God. And we will listen to music and ponder on the greatest gift: Jesus. As the harmony of carols fills our home, may we be attuned to the harmony God has sent in the Person of His Son, born to us, born for us, to give His life that we might be reconciled to Himself. Merry? No. Not really. But grateful and blessed? Yes.

"And she will bring forth a Son and you shall call His name JESUS, for He will save His people from their sins." Matthew 1:21. It's not stretching it to announce that the signpost for this day is **GIFTS.** And we will celebrate every one of them.

DOORS

Time is passing quickly heading for my big day. This week I need to go to "joint camp," which is a whole day of acquainting myself with the necessary knowledge for orthopedic surgery. Learning how to find my way around the hospital, how to prepare for surgery, what I need to know about afterward--that kind of knowledge. I guess I am feeling a bit more confident about the whole thing though still scared. But the sun is shining today and I feel God's love shining, too.

. . .

Someone sent a little quote on Facebook. "When life shuts a door, open it again. It's a door, that's how they work." There's a measure of truth there, even as it is spoken in Scripture in Matthew 7:7, "Ask, and it will be given to you; seek, and you will find; knock, and it will be opened to you." I tend to leave doors of unmet expectations closed, considering an opportunity I assumed was in front of me as no longer available. Perhaps it needs to be pursued a bit more until it's clearer that it's finished. I know I give up too easily; too quickly discouraged, my faith in what I thought was my ministry shredded, because I haven't been *successful*--not in the way I define it, anyway. Realizing that God may have used me in ways of which I am not aware, I still admit I have an unhealthy longing for recognition. It is one of the things that I need to surrender to Him.

This door of surgery ahead of me seems threatening. I am not ready to open it. A new year is here and it is a portal to be walked through. The discipline of keeping a journal that has been my spiritual mainstay now finds me reluctant to begin a new one for this year with all its crisp, white, empty pages. Why? Because my thoughts are consumed with the fact that I will be letting a surgeon cut me and replace a very painful joint with a metal one. Anxiety looms, and no matter what I tell myself about trusting God, there's a knot of fear inside that I can't seem to untie.

My sister voiced a possibility of what I fear--that if something goes wrong I'll be a cripple for life. But as Fred not-so-gently reminded me, I already *am* a cripple! The thing is, I feel guilty and wimpy when others have faced so many worse things.

May God grant me the courage to open the **DOORS** that I face with the grace only supplied by Him. What is waiting behind those doors is no surprise to Him. May this be a lesson of learning to trust, which I hope to learn well.

TRUST

Greetings. Today I want to talk about a topic I've discussed a bit over the past few weeks. It is my signpost for this week, a necessary one--**TRUST**. I attended a class called "joint camp" at the hospital, which did alleviate some of my anxiety. Although relieved in some areas, I think I am more worried about the after care than the actual surgery. All the advice rattles around in my head--what I must do, what I must not do, how to get out of bed, out of a chair, getting all the exercises and physical therapy. These things are weighing on my mind.

My tendency when troubled is to search God's Word for reassurance, so I turned to familiar passages. I want to share them with you, because who knows? You might need them too. "Whenever I am afraid, I will trust in You." Psalm 56:3. And later in this chapter, "Vows made to You are binding upon me, O God; I will render praises to You. For You have delivered my soul from death. Have You not kept my feet from falling that I may walk before God in the land of the living?" Psalm 56:11-12. Oh, I am chagrined to read these words reminding me of all God has already done! I love the way He prompts me to consider Him. I simply must TRUST.

These verses hang on my bathroom wall. "Our soul waits for the LORD; He is our help and our shield. For our heart shall rejoice in Him, because we have trusted in His holy name. Let Your mercy, O LORD, be upon us, just as we hope in You." Psalm 33:20-2. I will TRUST.

I close today with a prayer sent to me by my sister on the eve of my heart surgery. It speaks my newly trusting heart: "Lord, have mercy. Thee we adore. Into Thy hands. Amen."

SCARS

Greetings on this last day, pre-surgery. Tomorrow is the DAY. My journaling has been sporadic. Somehow I haven't been able to put words together because I'm dealing with conflicting emotions--faith and fear, expectation and fear of disappointment. I wrote the following piece a few years back, but as I have been pondering the upcoming surgery, I have been reminded of this expression of what I was feeling and am feeling again. Let me share it with you. It was written when I had another physical crisis, but the same issues prevail now. Can I, will I, trust? I am determined to do so, as I mentioned last week. God has been near, comforting me with His word, but I am still asking you to stand with me in prayer that His will be done in me. Thank you.

Here then is the signpost for this week. It's taken from something I did a long time ago, which I called **SCARS**. I am again appropriating these sentiments this week.

The doctor said if I would trust him with my care
he could relieve my pain, perhaps even take it away.
I should be leaping with delight.
Instead I lie here swallowing panic.
I wonder why?

Could it be that I love my pain?
Is it possible that it has become such a
familiar companion that I dare not let it go
lest I no longer have it to define me?
Have I used my pain as an excuse?
I think, though, that I fear to trust the doctor;
what if my hope is high and it doesn't work?
So here I lie, indecisive.

And I wonder about the pain of sin in my life--
hurt, anguish, betrayal, disappointment,
along with physical, chronic pain,
to which I cling in spite of myself.

The reality is that I'm emphasizing the scars
from my wounds, afraid to apply the
soothing balm that would heal my soul.
What would it be like to live pain free?

And what will it be like to live sin free?
I will know that actuality someday.
Until then, however, I will carry scars,
physical, emotional, spiritual scars.
Jesus, You died to heal my wounds.
If I accept Your healing work,
will You take my scars and turn them into
beauty marks?

Just think, the next time I will be writing you I'll have a
brand new hip. Hallelujah! "The LORD your God in your midst,
the Mighty One, will save; He will rejoice over you with gladness,
He will quiet you with His love, He will rejoice over you with
singing." Zephaniah 3:17.

RESTORATION

It's Groundhog Day! And I feel a little like the groundhog Punxutawney Phil, whose peeking up from the earth on this day seemingly predicts the length of winter we face. I feel like Phil because I am just poking my head above ground in many ways. I stumbled through January with the aid of a walker, a cane, my recliner, and oh yes, pain meds and physical therapy. I haven't communicated on social media, and for that I apologize. Somehow I just couldn't find my thoughts working in a way that would make sense to anyone.

It's been a long journey, but praise God, I am beginning to feel like myself again. I have a new hip as promised a month ago when last I posted. I am grateful; grateful to be on the mend, deeply thankful for the prayers that have upheld me through this process of surgery and healing. Thank you, all you who prayed and let me know you were praying. I am also thankful to Fred for the patient help and care he has given. I've been totally helpless, unable even to get a cup of coffee from the pot to my chair. He has been there every moment and I cannot thank God enough for him.

I choose "One Perfect Word" each year that I believe God plants in my heart and mind, and uses to demonstrate His love and care and promises. This year I picked **RESTORATION.**

For the past two years I have really struggled with health issues, and this has impacted so much of my life--who I am, what I'm to be doing, etc. Throughout this year I'll be praying that God will begin to restore our relationship; the relationship with Himself I've previously enjoyed, but which has been challenged in so many ways. I cling to His promise, in the book of Joel, chapter 2, verse 25a: "For I will restore to you the years the swarming locusts have eaten…"And further, in verses 26 and 27, "You shall eat in plenty and be satisfied, and praise the name of the LORD your God, who has dealt wondrously with you; and my people shall never be put to shame. Then you shall know that I in the midst of Israel: I am the LORD your God and there is no other. My people shall never be put to shame."

I realize this was a promise to His children Israel, but I also believe He gives this promise even today to His people, like me, who have struggled with issues of rebellion and doubt. You know, I've been challenged by the first syllable of my word for the year: *rest.* How very important it is.

Let me quote part of the February 1st entry from *The Listening Heart*[xxxvi], by Judy Gordon Morrow, (my devotional for 2016). She expresses so beautifully the way Jesus spoke to her, and I take great comfort from these words: "Rest in Me. You have come through some difficult times, some trying times, and now I need you to rest in Me. Let Me restore you. Let Me bring sweet healing to your spirit and soul. I have seen and known your pain and now I am covering you with the peace of My presence. I have allowed you to taste of deep pain, and your heart has enlarged in its capacity for compassion."[xxxvii]

Let the **RESTORATION** begin! I welcome you to be part of this journey.

BECKONING

Greetings! I feel I would like to expand a bit on the post from last week on rest and restoration. I am struggling again. I haven't written much lately, even in my journal. My mind feels sluggish and even my handwriting doesn't feel familiar. However, I have to begin once more examining this road to recovery upon which God has placed me. Journaling has always helped before to capture the intimacy with God that seems to beckon like a will-o-the-wisp. "Will-o-the-wisp" is defined as something that is difficult or impossible to find, reach or catch. I really don't like to use that term in connection with God, because He is well able to be reached and found. It is I who pulls away, rejecting the beckoning call. It is the word BECKON that intrigues me this morning. One definition is to use a hand gesture to call someone to you. But how about the synonyms? Much more ethereal, for example: charm, entice, attract, draw.

How does God beckon me? Because He *does*--not with a hand wave or gesture, but with His Word--phrases that catch my attention, call to remembrance, or perhaps echoes that remind and stir my heart's yearning for more. A pastor once spoke about the longing we have for more of God if we have ever really tasted Him. And I guess that's sort of where I am right now--aware and longing for Him like a thirsty land does. It is an ache that can only be satisfied by prolonged time in the Word. It is that to which God is beckoning me and my rest cannot begin until I give myself to Him. Matthew 11:28. "Come to Me, all you who labor and are heavy laden, and I will give you rest."

How about you? Is there a longing inside that only He can fill? Become aware, and answer His loving, beckoning personal Word. **BECKONING**--my signpost for the week.

PROGRESS

My friends, I write from an incredibly grateful heart this week. First of all, I am improving daily (having graduated from the walker to a cane), and today my therapist said I may begin to walk around the house without even that. Plus he did a progress report for me to take to the surgeon on Monday and said my improvement has been impressive. I remarked to Fred on the way home, "I can't help but be a little happy with myself." I have worked hard and I can definitely see results--a real avenue for praise.

Why is gratitude spilling out of me, you may wonder? I didn't mention it last week, but I was tasked to speak at four separate luncheons this week. They were all close to home, so no long travel, but still...only four and a half weeks out from hip surgery? I had serious doubts about my ability to complete all these commitments this week, but I had promised, and stated "I *will* do it, even if they have to carry me in!"

Well, praise God, I walked in, perched on a stool, and shared the Gospel and my own story with a lot of women. Gratitude for so many things makes me almost speechless in trying to communicate it. God's amazing enabling strength and power, as I experienced it repeatedly: the way the audiences were so gracious and accepting of my fumbling with cane and stool, the affirmations and encouragement, safe travel and Fred's sweet patience in doing all he could to be there for me in every way. Whew! That's a lot of stuff to be thankful for.

Earlier this week in my devotional reading and journaling, I came upon a verse in Psalm 29:11, which has long been a favorite. Somehow though, seeing a precious verse with new eyes gives it renewed impact. Here it is (and it actually sits on my kitchen window sill, so I *should* notice it every day): "The Lord will give

strength to His people; the Lord will bless His people with peace."
It has blessed me many times.

But oh what a chord it struck in me this day, as I was so
needy. A wonderful contrast--strength and peace, against my
weakness and agitation. I clutched that promise close all week,
depending on the strength that poured through me; strength that
overpowered the pain and could only have come from God. And
best of all, peace; the sweet peace that I was sitting (sometimes
standing) in His presence at each location. Yes, I am grateful.

The week is over. My prayer is that hearts were touched
and moved, because mine certainly was. I give all the praise and
glory to my God and Savior. If my name crossed your mind on
occasion and you lifted me up in prayer, I thank you. How
wonderfully those prayers were answered.

More good news: I have found my pen again. My journal
now has filled pages and I am finding excitement in what God has
in store over the next weeks.

THE CLIMB

Well, as usual after a time of great victory and rejoicing, things tend to fall flat. It's been a rough time lately.

At my physical therapy there is a poster with this quote, "The higher the goal, the more difficult the journey, and the sweeter the success." When I first read it, I thought, "That is so true." As I read it again the other day, I realized it anew. The journey to healing has many roadblocks it seems, hence, my signpost: **THE CLIMB.** It is two months post-surgery, and I am still walking with a cane, even though I am a lot better.

I can't say the same for Fred. He is not tolerating his immuno-therapy very well, and is suffering some miserable side effects. There is pain in all his joints and a burning sensation all over his body. Every movement is painful. It is to be expected apparently because the doctor's response, "Take Tylenol and we'll see you next week," makes it sound normal. But no one had ever mentioned this side effect and we didn't expect it. So now the Nurse has become the Nursed, as I am having to take care of him now like he has cared for me for months. It is a privilege, but I am exhausted and not sleeping well.

Therefore this week, I don't have much that is uplifting to share. I am writing, however, to request your prayers for us. As Fred remarked the other day, "God must know what He is doing. He waited until you were well enough to tend me before He allowed another bump in the road." There is acceptance in that, and we are resting in His care, grateful that I can drive now and do the errands, get to therapy and doctor's appointments. I'm thankful that we can see the end (he only has two more treatments), and looking forward to rejoining the lives we call "before."

May God bless you richly as you hold us up before the

Throne of Grace. And we would be happy to pray for you, especially if you are facing a climb of your own. Remember God's Word from Psalm 121:1-2, "I will lift up my eyes to the hills — from whence comes my help? My help comes from the LORD, who made heaven and earth." Oh, doesn't that bring comfort? The Maker of the mountains gives strength to climb them. And the view from the top is stupendous! He promised.

THE LOVE OF GOD

We are nearing the end. Recovery is in sight. I'm happy to say that this week has been brighter than last week with my dismal whining. My appointment with the surgeon revealed a lot of bone growth. Yippee! The pain is much less so I'm close to being back to normal.

My husband, however, still needs prayer. The doctor has elected not to continue his immuno-therapy treatments because of the severity of his reaction to it. We are hopeful, then, that four instillations of the vaccine will be sufficient to prevent the return of the cancer. In the meantime, we are so grateful that there won't be any more treatments--at least not for three months, when we return for another evaluation. Fred is still miserable, though, with the burning sensations traveling his body.

Thankfully we can see light at the end of the tunnel. It hasn't been an entirely dark tunnel, because God has been ever near, and we have had the light of His love showered all around us. I have been thinking of some of my favorite hymns lately, as I've been pondering all that has happened and struggling to word my response to His love. One day I found this quote from Judy Gordon Morrow in her book, *The Listening Heart*.[xxxviii] "All the ink in the world is woefully inadequate to pen the wonder of God's love."[xxxix] Naturally the words to the hymn, "The Love of God"[xl] moved into my awareness. Here are those lyrics for you: "If we with ink the ocean fill, and were each man a scribe by trade; were every stalk on earth a quill, and all the sky of parchment made; to write the love of God above would drain the ocean dry; nor could the scroll contain the whole, though stretched from sky to sky."[xli]

And my response, inscribed in my journal: "What incredible thoughts expressed so beautifully. They are enough to sustain and encourage my soul this day."

May **THE LOVE OF GOD** be your sustaining power as it is most definitely my signpost this week. His love was enough to send His Son to redeem us, and it is enough to stand upon and celebrate, even when a dark tunnel approaches. Oh, how precious it is to know that His love surrounds us! I am singing with every breath.

COMPASSION

Greetings. Today must not go without remark. It is exactly three months since my hip replacement. It's hard to believe that much time has passed! My recovery has not exactly met my expectations, as I had planned to be dancing in the streets by now. I can't do that yet, but I *am* walking on the sidewalks and crying out in gratitude to God for the healing that He and I have accomplished through my physical therapist.

I'm feeling almost my old self--perhaps a softer, more compassionate self. At least I hope so. Using a walker, a cane and depending on others can make a self-sufficient person like I was comprehend some of what many others go through. Sometimes we need a jolt to realize just how blessed we are. I know I did.

It's getting close to the 2nd year anniversary of the heart surgery. I am doing a lot of thinking about just what has gone on in my life lately, and am feeling my way back to the intimate relationship I previously enjoyed with God. It's different now--*I'm* different now. I am exploring the differences and attempting to discern just what He has ahead for me in the coming months. I pray that I will hear His guiding voice, and moreover, be obedient to it. I'm excited! It's so wonderful to feel good again. I can't express strongly enough how I appreciate the support and encouragement of your love and prayers throughout this journey. Let's keep walking and looking upward together.

Also, let's live with **COMPASSION** as we look not only upward, but outward toward others upon whom we can pour the compassion gained from facing and surmounting our trials. For, as the psalmist says in Psalm 86:15. "But You, O Lord, are a God full of compassion, and gracious." So we must be as well.

TIME

We are headed to our son's home this week, looking forward to having some good family time, celebrating our granddaughter's 18th birthday and her high school graduation. It does not seem possible that our grandchildren have already grown up and changed so much.

We are grateful, however, for the relationships that we have with them. It is also a joy to have a bit of a vacation. We are thanking God for the fresh air and for feeling well again--healthy after surgeries with the ability to get back into living. Also we are thankful for all the support and sweet wishes we have received. God is good!

I'm choosing **TIME** as my signpost this week. It seems to me that we moan the passing of time as something to be sorry for. I do, and I'm sure I'm not alone. We long to keep things the same, with hands raised, stiff-arming the clock and calendar, wishing for what can never be again.

On the other hand, we look forward in anticipation, as I have, to healing and growth, changes that will be improvements in our lives. Is this not a dichotomy? To moan about the passage of time while at the same longing for the things that only the future might bring? The psalmist says so clearly in Psalm 103:14-17a. "For He knows our frame; He remembers that we are dust. As for man, his days are like grass; as a flower of the field, so he flourishes. For the wind passes over it and it is gone, and its place remembers it no more. But the mercy of the LORD is from everlasting to everlasting, on those who fear Him..."

This brings me up short, especially when I get so involved in each present day. It is eternity with which we need be more concerned. This life is as grass that in eternal terms goes quickly and fades in the light of eternity--for which we were truly created.

164

Our humanity demands that time be our servant, working to bring about our goals and desires. But in God's economy, eternity is just beginning. So as I look at Psalm 103 and recognize my own frailty, I know that I want to cherish my past life while looking forward eagerly to what God has in store for my eternal future. I do not want to be a slave to time, but to celebrate it whether it seems to pass quickly or drag. As they say, time is relative, and I love to notice that each day is one day closer to heaven!

MEMORIAL

At last! I have reached a resting place on my journey. Two years ago my life changed when my faulty arteries were repaired and my heart restored. I will always remember and celebrate that date, and I invite you all to celebrate with me in praising God for His intervention and subsequent care of me.

Often a milestone or anniversary begs reflection. We look back over the journey, assessing what we have learned, how we have changed and where we go from here. I am reflecting not only on the heart surgery, but the hip replacement, the gout, the dehydration event, Fred's cancer--all of which are the steps I have traveled on my journey.

My signpost for this week, as I want to consider the events leading up to today, is **MEMORIAL**. In ancient biblical times, it was customary to set up some sort of physical reminder of how God had blessed His people. In fact, Joshua was ordered by God to have twelve men, one from each tribe, take a stone from the middle of the Jordan River and carry it to the other side to set up a memorial so that the descendants would know the wonder-filled miracles God performed in their behalf. In Joshua 4:7 the scripture says, "Tell them that the flow of the Jordan was cut off before the ark of the covenant of the LORD. When it crossed the Jordan, the waters of the Jordan were cut off. These stones are to be a memorial to the people of Israel forever."

This book, *Signposts,* is my memorial. It signifies the pause in the journey to remember and reflect on the ways God has touched my life and showed me Himself.

I feel I am almost recovered at this point and I want to let everyone know that what is uppermost in my thoughts today is a profound sense of deep gratitude. I had blithely sailed along for most of my life, taking health and God's blessings for granted. No more. Each day is a treasure for which I whisper *thank you* to my Heavenly Father, along with a prayer to be used however He can use me, because my life has definitely been saved more than once in the past two years.

It is also incumbent on me to relate the sense of renewal that comes from the remembering, the reflection. It creates a new commitment to draw even closer to God through His Word, to be bolder in sharing Him, fulfilling my life's purpose--which is to know Him and then to make Him known. That is the purpose for all of us who are His children. No matter how that plays out for each one of us, it is why we are still here on earth. And I know this for certain because I am still alive, realizing how easily I might not have been. This, my friends, is renewal.

So, "Here I raise my Ebenezer, hither by Thy help I'm come,"[xlii] as the old hymn says. Here today I set up the stones, the words that have moved my own heart and that I have shared with my readers.

Thank you for your presence in my life, and on my journey.

FORWARD

Greetings! Where do I go from here? What happens next? I have been pondering this, knowing that this particular season of my odyssey is coming to an end. I have a new place of understanding that I would never have reached without the ups and downs and the paths, both rough and smooth, along the way.

It was no coincidence this morning when I opened my devotional book, *The Listening Heart* by Judy Gordon Morrow and found this quote from J. C. Ryle, written in the late 1800's: "Whether you are weak or strong, in the valley or on the mount, in sickness or in health, in sorrow or in joy--in youth or in age, in richness or in poverty, in life or in death—let this be your motto and guide, 'LOOKING UNTO JESUS.'"[xliii]

And the scripture that immediately springs to mind next is Hebrews 12:1-2: "Therefore we also, since we are surrounded by so great a cloud of witnesses, let us lay aside every weight, and the sin which so easily ensnares us, and let us run with endurance the race that is set before us, **looking unto Jesus**, the author and finisher of our faith, who for the joy that was set before Him endured the cross, despising the shame, and has sat down at the right hand of the throne of God."

The answer to my earlier question of where to go from here is this: **FORWARD**--ever forward into a deeper relationship with Him, letting Him guide my steps. You, my readers and prayer partners, as a big part of my "great cloud of witnesses" have blessed me immeasurably. I pray that always, whatever happens, you and I will be looking unto Jesus. I am so grateful to you and I celebrate you and your sweet encouragement and care, as I shout praise to our awesome God.

ACKNOWLEDGMENTS

Putting together a book of this nature is dependent on so many things: concentration, discipline, commitment. All of which would be impossible without the incredible support of my family: my sons and their families, and particularly my husband, Fred. He is a gift to me in innumerable ways--loving me through the wilderness times, cheering for me in the times of fullness. My loved ones are invaluable to me and I am very grateful.

I want to thank Krista Dunk, as well, for her unfailingly wise and helpful work with me on the publishing end--for her loving assistance and faithful prayers.

And my pastors! They will never know how their messages impact my heart. God has used them many times. Speaking unadulterated truth from the pulpit, they have helped me find courage and hope from God's Word when I have been close to faltering.

There isn't enough space anywhere to list the names of those who have been so faithful to walk with me on my journey. Friends who have read the manuscript and said, "Go for it!" Also, I would be remiss in my acknowledgments without a giant THANKS to those who have helped to proofread and edit this book, as well as readers who have prayed and commented on my blog, letting me know that what God teaches me has touched them as well. I hope you all know who you are and will rejoice with me on this finished product, aware that your prayers and support are of inestimable value. May God bless you in every way!

ABOUT THE AUTHOR

Lois Williams makes her home at Jubilee, an active adult community in Lacey, WA, with her husband, Fred. Lois is a poet and a speaker. As an author, Lois has a way with words that captivates her audiences and helps them see God's Word in a new light. Her books flow with personal realities and power from the Holy Spirit with every day, ordinary life experiences to open one's heart to feel God's love and sometimes His necessary rebuke. A poet who composes a journal of intimacy between herself and God, using it as a tool for developing a deeper relationship with God and celebrating the freedom it brings.

Visit Lois' website to learn more about her books and speaking schedule at **www.LoveLettersFromLois.com**.

ENDNOTES

[i] Sarah Young, *Jesus Calling* © 2004 (Thomas Nelson Inc.) p. 122

[ii] Babbie Mason, quoted in Women of Faith Devotional Bible, Copyright © 2003, by Thomas Nelson, Inc. p. 80

[iii] R. Kelso Carter, "Standing On The Promises", *Baptist Hymnal,* © 1975, Convention Press, p. 335

[iv] The Afters, "Broken Hallelujah", Lyrics © 2013 Dan Ostero, Jordan Mohilowski, Matthew D. Fuqua @ Music Services, Inc.

[v] Ibid.

[vi] Vonette Bright, quoted in Women of Faith Devotional Bible.

[vii] Ibid.

[viii] Debbie Macomber, *One Perfect Word,* Copyright © 2012 (Howard Books, A Divisison of Simon & Schuster, Inc.

[ix] Bryan Duncan, "Bryan's Song Hymn (When I Turn To You)." Lyrics, Bryan Duncan and James Felix, Copyright © 1996 Fanatic Music, by Word Inc./Word Music, a Div. of Word, Inc.

[x] Ibid.

[xi] Sarah Young, *Jesus Calling, p. 250*

[xii] Quote attributed to Winston Churchill, British Statesman, 1874-1965

[xiii] Jan Silvious, quoted in Women of Faith Devotional Bible, p. 168

[xiv] Kathy Troccoli, Stubborn Love. Lyrics Amy Grant, Gary Chapman, Sloan Towner, Brown Bannister& Michael W. Smith. Copyright © 1982 Bases Loaded Music/ Meadowgreen Music Co. (ASCAP)

[xv] Ibid.

[xvi] The Message, Copyright © 2002 by Eugene H. Peterson

[xvii] Barbara Johnson, as quoted in Women of Faith Devotional Bible, p. 774

[xviii] Priscilla J. Owens, "We Have An Anchor", *Great Hymns of the Faith,* p. 265 Copyright © 1968 by Singspiration, Inc., p.

[xix] Daniel W. Whittle, 1883 "There Shall be Showers of Blessing,", *Baptist Hymnal,* p. 273

[xx] Sarah Young, *Jesus Calling,* p. 49

[xxi] Ibid.

[xxii] William Shakespeare, *Macbeth,* Act II, Scene ii

[xxiii] Emily Dickinson, *No. 254 (Copyright © 1861)*

[xxiv] Sarah Young, *Jesus Calling,* p. 83

[xxv] Helen Lemmel, "Turn Your Eyes Upon Jesus", Copyright © 1922, *Baptist Hymnal,* p. 198

[xxvi] Dee Brestin, as quoted in Women of Faith Devotional Bible, p. 639

[xxvii] Holley Gerth, Author, in "Coffee For Your Heart" blog post 4/15/15

[xxviii] Ibid.

[xxix] Nicole Johnson, quoted in Women of Faith Devotional Bible, p. 1505
[xxx] Frances R. Havergal, "Take My Life And Let It Be", (1874), *Baptist Hymnal*, p. 373
[xxxi] Patsy Clairmont, quoted in Women of Faith Devotional Bible, p. 793
[xxxii] Charles H. Spurgeon, (1834-1892), 991.282 Quote from "Exploring the Mind and Heart of the Prince of Preachers
[xxxiii] Richard C. Halvorson, (1916-1995), Former Senate Chaplain.
[xxxiv] Mercy Me, "Word of God Speak", Lyrics, Bart Millard & Pete Kipley, Copyright © Warner/Chappell Music, Inc./Music Services, Inc.
[xxxv] Ibid.
[xxxvi] Judy Gordon Morrow, *The Listening Heart*, Copyright © 2013 Judy Gordon Morrow, in association with the literary agency of WordServe Literary Group.
[xxxvii] Ibid. p. 50
[xxxviii] Judy Gordon Morrow, *The Listening Heart.*
[xxxix] Ibid. p. 82
[xl] Frederick M. Lehman (1868-1953) "The Love of God", Copyright © 1923, Ren. 1951 by Hope Publishing Co., Carol Stream, IL
[xxx] Ibid.
[xli] Ibid.
[xlii] Robert Robinson, "Come Thou Fount of Every Blessing", (1758), *Baptist Hymnal*, p. 13
[xliii] Judy Gordon Morrow, *The Listening Heart*, p. 132

Signposts Proudly Published by:

Creative Force Press

www.CreativeForcePress.com

Do You Have a Book in You?

Made in the USA
San Bernardino, CA
06 January 2019